T0131660

Revealing My Story

FROM DARKNESS TO GLORY

DR. CHRISTINE LANDRY ELLIOTT

WESTBOW
PRESS®
A DIVISION OF THOMAS NELSON
& ZONDERVAN

WestBow Press books may be ordered through booksellers or by contacting:

WestBow Press
A Division of Thomas Nelson & Zondervan
1663 Liberty Drive
Bloomington, IN 47403
www.westbowpress.com
844-714-3454

ISBN: 978-1-6642-5527-2 (sc)
ISBN: 978-1-6642-5526-5 (hc)
ISBN: 978-1-6642-5528-9 (e)

Library of Congress Control Number: 2022900646

Print information available on the last page.

WestBow Press rev. date: 03/15/2022

Dedication

First, I dedicate this book to my Lord and Savior, Jesus Christ, who has destined me to author this book for kingdom purpose. Secondly, I dedicate this book to my parents, Ruth Landry, and the late Harold Landry. My father always showed me love and provided me with the fundamental principles that have empowered me to take on the challenges of life. My mother has been the most loving mother and the greatest influence throughout my life journey. Mom, thank you for never giving up on me, and for always standing firm on the promises of God concerning my destiny.

In memory of my children who have transitioned, Yolanda and Travis; you will always be in my heart, and I think about you two often. To the daughter, the Lord has allowed me to still have on this earth, Teresa, my "chosen child." I pray my story will reveal a greater understanding of unanswered questions and reveal a brighter light into your journey that is leading you to your divine purpose. Just know I love you and I am so proud of the beautiful and successful lady you have become. I decree and declare that you will walk into your divine purpose and destiny for the kingdom of God.

I also dedicate my book to my grand-daughter, Keosha, to my grandsons Pierre, Brendell, and Duron; and in memory of Breon, who passed away in the year of 2020. To my siblings and all my nieces and nephews, thank you for your support, prayers, and love

Contents

Foreword

Transformation: a thorough or dramatic change in form or appearance.

That is what comes to mind when I think of the life, legacy, and personage of Christine Landry Elliott. I have known her since the mid-1970s, but she and my wife have been friends, neighbors, and church friends since childhood.

Christine's life story is a testament of the redeeming power of the blood of Jesus. We have been intricately involved in each stage of her development, from spiritual infancy to the informed warrior for Christ. We have witnessed audiences travel an emotional journey as Christine shared a portion of her testimony in radio interviews, intimate conversations, counseling sessions, and revivals.

Christine is a gift to the body of Christ, and her story will inspire her readers to a new place of faith and hope for their lost loved ones.

Dr. John L. and Ms. Vertell T. Godbolt
Partners in Marriage, Inc.
www.partnersinmarriage.com

Preface

As a new author, I am so grateful to God to have this opportunity to birth this book about my personal story after going astray from my Christian upbringing and moral values. I experienced near-death experiences resulting from my drug addiction, my illicit activities, my criminal involvement, being a rape and domestic violence victim, and confined in prison, but now I am a transformed Christ follower. This was the pathway God allowed me to go through after overcame by a spirit of rebellion and drifting into the depth of sin. I thank God for His grace and mercies that sustained me through the miseries of my sins and preserved my life for kingdom purpose.

I share my story in total transparency and unashamedly because today I am a new creature and spiritually transformed by the power of the blood of Jesus Christ.

According to 2 Corinthians 5:17 (KJV), "Therefore, if any man be in Christ, he is a new creature: old things are passed away; behold, all things are become new." I am a witness that the blood still works!

I want my story to inspire and encourage mothers whose children have strayed away from their Christian upbringing and Christian values. I want to share how the power of my mother's prayers and faith interceded on my behalf when I was close to death's door. When I lost all strength and hope, my mother held onto the horns of the altar, wailing and travailing, praying against the strongholds that held me hostage and almost took my soul to hell. My mother's prayers ran me down, and God sent His angelic hosts to arrest me and return me home safely. What intended to kill me and take me to a burning hell, God delivered me and turned my misery into ministry for kingdom purpose.

I pray my book will encourage that mother and that father to not lose faith, and to not let the devil have their seed, their chosen child! Fight the good fight of faith.

I also pray that my testimony will inspire and speak to the hearts of this young generation who have strayed from good morals and value system and their Christian upbringing. I believe God has called this "Joshua generation" to conqueror, possess, and rule over what is rightfully the people of God.

As one who survived in the streets, I engaged in illicit behaviors; as one addicted to drugs, I was a drug supplier; I did other illicit behaviors, and I served prison time for armed robbery. As a result of these activities, I suffered from near-death encounters. Every experience had to do with seeking my identity and acceptance and trying to fill voids in my life that only God can fill. I had issues with self-love and a need for acceptance. I brought pain and shame to my family and especially to my children. The devil's intention was to destroy me before I reached my destiny that God had predestined for me. Thank God for the blood of Jesus Christ and His sacrifices made at Calvary, and for His resurrection power that reconciled us back to our heavenly Father.

The thief cometh not, but for to steal, and to kill, and to destroy: I am come that they might have life, and that they might have it more abundantly. (John 10:10 KJV)

I do not care how far down you have fallen; God's hand is not too short to pull you out and transform your life.

That if thou shalt confess with thy mouth the Lord Jesus,
and shalt believe in thine heart that God hath raised him from the dead,
thou shalt be saved. For with the heart man believeth
unto righteousness; and with the mouth confession is
made unto salvation. (Romans 10:9–10 KJV)

Acknowledgments

To my husband, Bishop George Henry Elliott, who has been my motivator and an encourager throughout the process of authoring my book. You have enhanced my life both personally and spiritually. I would have never pursued my master's degree in counseling, a licensed addiction specialist in the field of substance abuse therapy, or my doctoral degree in ministry without your encouragement and support, which has enhanced my personal growth in capacities. I thank you and love you.

A special salute and a big thank you to Bishop John and Vertell Godbolt. Words could never express the depth of my love I have for you two. I appreciate your teachings and words of wisdom, that both empowered and enhanced my spiritual and personal growth. Bishop Godbolt, I will never forget the word of life you preached and the labor you invest to pull my soul out of sin the night I surrendered my life to God. Since the day of my conversion, Bishop John, and Elect Lady Vertell Godbolt, you have served as my spiritual advisors, my mentors, my coach, my prayer warriors, and you are my friends. During the most challenging times of my Christian journey, you were always there to encourage me and speak life.

Thanks to my spiritual leader and spiritual father who affirmed me into ministry, the late Bishop William Townsend.

A special thanks to Dr. Tangula Diggs, who encouraged me throughout the process in authoring this book.

A special thanks to Minister Michael and LaCinda Fuller of MRF Graphic and Music, who assisted me with the preparation for the publication process.

Introduction

As I reflect on the years of my life, I have so much gratitude to my Lord and Savior, Jesus Christ, for snatching me from many near-death experiences, a life of sin, and condemnation to hell. My life's journey began as a church girl who abandoned her religious upbringing, and that resulted in me becoming a high school dropout, a drug addict, a woman of the night, a criminal, a rape and domestic violence victim, a homeless person, and an inmate in prison. Now I am a beneficiary of His glory. I am grateful because I am born-again and transform by the power of the blood of Jesus Christ. I am a Christ follower. I pray my story will be instrumental in inspiring others to transform their lives and to give hope to the hopeless. From my experiences, I have a right to say: glory to God, glory hallelujah!

CHAPTER 1

Church Girl Goes Astray

He brought me up also out of an horrible pit,
out of the miry clay,
and set my feet upon a rock,
and established my goings.
(Psalm 40:2 KJV)

How do you manage your worries and fears about that child who has gone astray? As a parent and a grandparent of five children, I had to battle that fear and those concerns while they were growing up, and sometimes it was stressful. I feared them ending up in prison or worse, dying in the streets or dying alone due to negative influences and the enticement of the lusts of the flesh that can lead to the road of destruction. I was that young adult who strayed from my Christian upbringing and moral values, which led me into a riotous lifestyle.

My mother is a minister and is of the Pentecostal Holiness denomination. It is by the grace and mercies of God coupled with the prayers of my mother that I survived to tell my story. The power of my mother's intercession prayers, warring day and night, and fasting drove back demonic forces and drove back the spirit of death from over my life. My mother is a God-fearing woman and a prayer warrior who refused to allow the devil to have my soul. I am a living witness and living proof of the fact that when nothing else works, prayer will! The Word of God declares in James 5:16 (KJV), "The effectual fervent prayer of a righteous man availeth much." The Amplified Version of James 5:16 reads, "The heartfelt and persistent prayer of a righteous man (believer) is able to accomplish much [when put into action and made effective by God—it is dynamic and can have tremendous power]." This kind of prayer has the power to lose and bind up strongholds.

Both of my parents raised all eight of their children. They were not perfect, but they were loving, diligent workers, and excellent providers for their children. They made life bearable with what they had available. Our family time was at the kitchen table. No one could eat until dad received his serving first.

Today, I can appreciate the values and biblical standards my parents planted in my life. There were no discussions on real-life issues, such as womanhood, practical skills in dealing with life challenges, and dealing with emotions. Dad was quiet and very reserved, and he avoid dealing with conflicts among us but left it to mom to resolve. The number one rule in our house was, "Whatever is done in this house stays in this house!" So, there were family secrets and I learned to suppress emotions. We knew our parents loved all of us very much and would do anything to protect us from danger or harm. I recollect Mom getting up early in the mornings before daybreak to pray and to go out to work in the cotton field. Mom also worked as a housekeeper for local employers. I recall going to assist her one day and witnessing her challenging work as she scrubbed floors with her hands. Whatever Mom could do to bring extra money into the house, she would if it did not conflict with her church attendance.

When Mom went out to work or church, she depended on my sister and me to take care of the house. I was the oldest child, so I understood that maintaining the house was my responsibility. Now, as I think back, I missed enjoying my childhood. My mom attended church at least four days a week. There were five-night revival services, at least four times yearly; services would sometimes last until midnight. Dad worked Monday through Friday at a factory and later accepted a position with a local bus station. As a young adult, I felt resentment toward Dad because he was so reserved and passive in handling conflicts. Mom was the disciplinarian, and she took care of the house. Having any entertainment in the house, such as music or movies, that Mom perceived as sinful were unacceptable. We watched television, but all the shows were wholesome, such as Christian movies, cowboy shows, and game shows. Mom governed her house on the declaration made by the scripture according to the following:

And if it seem evil unto you to serve the LORD, choose you this day whom ye will serve; whether the gods which your fathers served that were on the other side of the flood, or the gods of the Amorites, in whose land ye dwell: but as for me and my house, we will serve the LORD. (Joshua 24:15 KJV)

There were no options about going to church. Sickness or having schoolwork to complete was not an excuse. Sometimes church services would last until midnight during school days, and we had to get up early the next morning. There were days we had to walk to school for miles, but we did it without complaining.

Train up a child in the way he should go: and when he is old, he will not depart from it. (Proverbs 22:6 KJV)

Mom instilled God's Word and wisdom in me, and it remained in me even when I had gone astray. Despite all the punishments and spankings, I never had any questions concerning Mom's love for me. Remembering my Christian upbringing and the power of my mother's prayers covered me and was the lifeline that snatched me out of what I call a "dark and miserable life of sin." God blocked all my near-death encounters. Today, I thank God for the exposure and foundational teaching I received from my parents and other spiritual leaders. I am grateful Mom did not make it an option to attend church, because it was the anchor that kept me grounded when I went astray. The seed of the Word was rooted inside and sustained me until I returned to the things of God.

As a young adult, I learned to conform and enjoy going to church because it became a way of life. The services were very animated, with those seasoned church mothers and fathers dancing in the spirit, singing those old gospel songs for about an hour, and running up and down the aisles with loud voices declaring victory and gratitude for the goodness of God. The testimony services were long but electrifying; we heard about miracles people experienced by the power of God. I remember seeing people walking into church on canes and crutches but walking out of church without them. It was nothing to walk into church to see crutches, canes, and neck braces hanging on the walls as evidence that the apostolic power had come through and healed people. The Spirit was thick in this small and wooden-floor church. People appeared to be on a natural high, being intoxicate by the spirit and staggering like a drunk man with the evidence of speaking in tongues. As the spirit moved, it stirred up the gift of prophecy. We reverenced the move of the Holy Spirit; no one moved until God spoke through His chosen servant. Back then, there were those prophets we called "woe prophets," who would forewarn the church of things God would reveal to them. I was afraid of two specific prophets who would get up and warn us of things to come. They would prophesy, "You'd better get it right or judgment!" We all would be still and tremble because we knew whatever they saw or spoke was about to happen.

I recall during a revival service when our pastor, Late Bishop Townsend, was about to give the benediction. One of the prophets, Mother Crecy, who has since transitioned to be with the Lord, stood up and started speaking in tongues (heavenly language). She started prophesying and warned us all, "Be careful! I see in the Spirit somebody in here getting in a car accident." Our pastor and the saints began to pray for traveling mercy and asked God to cover all of us with His shield of protection. As we left church, my mom decided she wanted a soda from the community store. We pulled up, and the brakes gave out on the car. Had it not been for the long soda box machine stationed outside the glass window, we would have run straight through the glass doors. The impact was so hard that we all jerked, but not injured. This happened less than fifteen minutes after the prophecy.

I experienced a real encounter with God, so there were not any doubts about God's existence and supernatural power. There was a reverence for the presence of God and the things of God. I heard unbelievers articulating fear of being in the presence of those church mothers and those Holy Ghost preachers. They feared their unrighteousness would be reveal to the prophets. Demons could not be at rest in the presence of God's anointed servants. I remember seeing and hearing demonic forces crying out and cast out under the power of God. I witnessed people being tormented by demons; those seasoned mothers and preachers pleaded the blood of Jesus

Christ over their lives. Every unclean spirit and stronghold were loosed from them, and they were delivered.

I came up in one of those tongue-talking, feet-stomping, and hand-clapping church of God. Those seasoned saints knew how to usher in the presence of God, pulling on the anointing until the glory of God filled the house. The move of God was so forceful, impactful, and contagious that the Spirit rested even upon the children. I really looked forward to the excitement of praising God and dancing in the spirit. Sometimes the glory of God would touch my spirit, and I would find myself crying.

I was at the age of nine or ten years old when I experienced my first personal encounter under the power of the Holy Spirit. They told me I would see in the Spirit realm and share the message from the angels and God. I would always jump up and down dancing in the Spirit with those older church mothers, enjoying the flow of the anointing and the anointed music. I remember of an encounter I experienced under a heavy outpouring of the Holy Spirit. I fell to the floor crying and rolling on the floor under the power of God. I got so drunk in the spirit that I could barely walk back to my seat. I blended in with those older saints dancing in the spirit at an early age. I knew at an early age that the Holy Spirit was inside me. I began to embrace the church and the beliefs of my mother's teaching. Mom shared with me of an encounter she had with God, when God ministered to her, "Christine is chosen and anointed for greatness"

Before I formed thee in the belly I knew thee; and before
thou camest forth out of the womb I sanctified thee,
and I ordained thee a prophet unto the nations.
(Jeremiah 1:5 KJV)

My mom would prophesy over my life and tell me often, "God is going to use you greatly!" Those preachers would preach those hell, fire, and brimstone messages, putting the fear of God in our hearts. They had us so scared about going to hell! They had us feeling like Jesus was coming that night! On Sundays, and during revivals, my church friends and I would go to the altar asking for forgiveness all over again because of condemnation of our sins. Those seasoned preachers made us feel so sinful and condemned about the smallest error we made. Even when we confessed salvation, we were already born-again (had sonship with God), and we were still saying, "Lord, save me some more!" Outside folks would call our Pentecostal denomination during those days "Holy Rollers." What they were suggesting was true because we did roll on the floor from the back of the church to the front or from the front to the back. During my upbringing, teaching was based on works, not too much on the grace of God. It was more religion and legalism, ("do this and don't do that") with little teaching on the mercies and grace of God.

There were so many prophetic words spoken over my life throughout my childhood, and the ones I heard the most were, "God has a special calling upon your life." Mom would tell me how so many times the devil tried to take my life while in her womb and after birth. She told me as a child, I battled with chronic asthma. Mom said that she spent countless hours in the emergency room because of my asthma. She told me that she took me to a campground healing and miracles tent meeting of a great evangelist, the Late A. A. Allen; we called him the Miracle Man because supernatural miracles happen under his tent ministry. It was at this campground revival that I received my healing from chronic asthma. The devil's plan was to kill me as an infant, but his tactics could not work because I was destined for kingdom purposes. God's chosen vessels are the devil's worst nightmare and are at the top of his hit list. I believe all of us have a calling for God's divine purpose if we surrender to His call. The devil desires to destroy all of us before we reach our destiny.

> St. John 10:10 (KJV) declares, "The thief cometh not, but for
> to steal, and to kill, and to destroy: I am come that they might
> have life, and that they might have it more abundantly."

I perceive that God's chosen vessels are those who are destined for greatness, as God destined Joseph as a "Preserver of Life" even though he had to have a "pit experience" to reach his destiny. God has a way to turn your misery into ministry!

> For I know the thoughts that I think toward you, saith the LORD,
> thoughts of peace, and not of evil, to give you an expected end.
> (Jeremiah 29:11 KJV)

I often relate my life experiences to the story in the Bible about the prodigal son. There are different perspectives of the story: The love of the father and the son that strayed away from his father's house to follow carnal desires. I am a witness that "the lust of the flesh, the lust of the eyes, and pride of life" (1 John 2:16 KJV) can alter the plans of God, which leads us into an end of disaster. This story testifies to the love of our Heavenly Father who loves us unconditionally even when we stray from His divine will for our lives. The story of the prodigal son allowed the lust of the flesh, lust of the eyes, and pride of life to drive him out of his father's house. The spirit of rebellion is as the spirit of witchcraft, an open door for demonic forces that will lead to deception and spiritual or physical death. This chosen child became the "odd one" of the family. I rebelled against my parent's standards and the will of God. It is amazing how sin can distort one's way of thinking and perception. The devil does not want us to know our value in the kingdom of God. We are "chosen," as God's masterpiece set aside for the master's plan. "For many are called, but few are chosen" (Matthew 22:14 KJV).

If you are reading this book, I decree and declare that you are one of His chosen ones! I always felt different and struggled to fit in with other peers, schoolmates, and those within our church circle. I did not understand then, but now I know I was a misfit because I was set aside for kingdom purpose. I felt deprived and thought everyone was having fun, had more freedom and was more popular than me. I was a victim of bullying and made fun of by classmates throughout my school years, even in high school. By the time I arrived in high school, my grades dropped. I was skipping school, hanging out with friends drinking, and flirting with boys. I became rebellious. Mom became firmer with restrictions and with her disciplinary actions. We lived in a poor community, but my parents would always find a way to meet our needs. We might not have had what we wanted, but we never went hungry. Mom and Dad planted a garden in the backyard. They planted corn, sweet potatoes, peas, collard greens, and other vegetables. I also remembered times we ate grits morning, noon, and at nights when money got tight. Our parents' love and prayers kept us together. Back in the days, like it is today, a person's socioeconomic status was determined based on where they lived and other external variables. We did not realize just how poor we were because the community we lived in was like a village, and everyone looked like us and we looked out for one another. Everybody's mom was everyone else's mom! Most people within our community attended the same church.

As I aged, I became resentful about having to attend church so much and not being able to go out to play with my friends. I had to wear those old grandma outfits that were hand-me-downs, or outfits mom stitched by hand or on her old sewing machine. She would dress us in long skirts and long sleeves tops that buttoned up to our neck. Every part of our bodies from the neck down had to be cover, even our legs. During those days, this was the dress code for Christian ladies in our denomination. I reckon they were trying to cover and protect us from demonic activities assigned to destroy and steal our virginity. I remembered my shoes were so old and worn out that there were holes in the bottom of them. I would put a piece of cardboard in the bottom to help keep my feet protected from cuts and rain. I loved the black and white penny loafers. Those loafers were popular, and although mine had holes in the bottom, I did not mind because I was walking in style. During my upbringing, those preachers and seasoned mothers believed it was a sin for women to wear pants, jewelry, and makeup, and they believed red was a representation of a Jezebel spirit (seductive spirit) as they interpreted it in those days. Hearing this did not help my self-esteem because I felt unattractive and had to look different from my peers in school. I remembered being a victim of bullying and called ugly names. All I desired was to feel like I fitted in, and I just wanted acceptance among the unchurched people. There was a void and an emptiness I felt. We could not go to the movies, we could not play certain games or sports, but there were minimal social activities that Mom allowed. The only activity done on Sundays was to attend church. Mom required her girls to have cooking and homemaking skills, so my sister, Evelyn, and I spent majority of time in the house cleaning and cooking.

During my early upbringing, my dad was not a follower of Christ, but he respected Mom's Christianity. Mom was very protective of her girls, warning us often that we should avoid entertaining boys and grown men. She always expressed how she loved us. Every weekend, she would go to town to buy us toys. They would be small games such as jack rocks, a jar of bubbles, coloring books, puzzles, and other games that would just cost a dollar, but mom gave them with love. During those days, getting toys was special, even those dollar deals, especially with my parent's income. Dad demonstrated his love indirectly through actions more so than saying, "I love you." Dad never forgot his children's birthdays. He always had at least five or ten dollars to give to us to celebrate our birthdays. Dad was very skillful in fixing things, repairing appliances and cars, plumbing, and doing other odd jobs. He was our personal fixer man. We all called him when things broke down and needed repairs. Dad was quiet and reserved. He enjoyed gambling, playing dice, and fishing. My brother Jeffery was his fishing partner.

Both of my parents shared stories about their parents during their childhood upbringing. My mother shared with me that her father was a preacher and was a very firm disciplinarian. I reckon he had an image to uphold as a preacher and a businessperson within his community. I never got a chance to meet my grandfather, but it sounded like he was a respected man within the community. Mom made it known that she was closer to her mother. I had an opportunity to get to know her, and I loved my grandmother. Grandmother had me feeling like I was her favorite grandchild. She had that kind effect on you when you were in her presence. All her grandchildren were her favorite. When she passed, I remembered feeling like I had lost my best friend and momma.

Dad, in contrast, did not know his father during his early childhood. He told me it was not until he was a grown man that he met a man who was supposed to have been his father. He only met him once. He identified his mother as an alcoholic and described his upbringing as 'challenging. Not any of us ever met my father's mother, not even my mom. Dad decided to join the military to escape from all the pain and challenges he faced at home. He was living with his grandmother prior to going into the military. Dad shared significant details of his upbringing with me when I was an adult, after inquiring consistently. One day while eating at a restaurant after returning from his doctor's appointment, he finally shared a portion of his story. I often wondered why he shared little emotions and affection. I knew Dad loved us; he simply never articulated it or embraced me with that hug that every little girl desires from her daddy.

Dad shared one of his saddest memories that made me sorrowful for him. The day of his departure for boot camp for the military, he went to tell his mother goodbye, but when he arrived, she was on the back porch drunk. She was too drunk to acknowledge his presence. He said he walked away heartbroken. He said that he tried to escape the memories of that day by leaving home. His mother eventually died from a medical condition related to her alcoholism.

I am grateful that neither Mom or Dad drank alcohol or used drugs. I would say that my mom was faithful and committed to her church and Christian beliefs. Dad's nonverbal communication spoke volumes. He was not perfect, but he was a good family-oriented person who loved mom and his children.

I was in my thirties when I put pressure on my father to say the words, "I love you." The little girl inside came alive! It is obvious by now that I was a daddy's girl. I was the oldest of eight children. When mom had his first son, Dad was so proud to have a son to take on his name. My siblings and I had a strong bond of love that kept us together. We all knew Mom's house rule and the consequences if we failed to comply. Cleaning the house, washing the clothes on the washboard, cooking, and attending to my siblings were still the responsibilities of my sister and me when Mom was away from home.

When I was around the age of seventeen, my rebellious and defiant behaviors increased, as evidenced by skipping school, grades dropping, going out to clubs, hanging out with soldiers, and staying out late or all night. Mom did not allow her girls to wear pants due to her religious beliefs. During my junior high school attendance, I would leave the house with a dress on and stash a pair of pants for later. When I planned to slip out of the house to hang out with friends, I would change into my pants. I wanted to blend in with their dress code. I became less concerned about Mom punishing me for disobeying her house rules. Dad did not confront my rebellious behaviors, but I knew he was not pleased. Even though I was staying out, I maintained my virginity. My mother put the fear of God in us about the possibility of getting pregnant if we were intimate with the other sex. Those old folks imparted so many myths about little boys touching the girls. They had us believing if you just kissed a boy, you could get pregnant. I continued to skip school, drinking, and experimenting with marijuana. My partying time was at clubs on the military base. I became more acquainted with military guys while hanging out at the club dancing. I was still staying in my mom's house and was on a curfew which I violated often.

I eventually dropped out of school in the eleventh grade. Peer pressure became overwhelming for me. No matter what I would do to try to fit into this group of associates it was never good enough. My relationships with my teachers were not good either. I always felt insecure around other girls that were outside our Christian community. I felt ugly and unprivileged because we were not as prosperous as others, and I struggled with lack of self-worth. I had this mindset that teachers did not embrace me as they did others, because of my looks and I dressed less stylish from the other girls. During my younger days, I felt inferior to others who was of another ethnicity. I always found myself looking for the back seat in the classroom. Feeling like a misfit was a norm for me. I desperately sought to get acceptance outside the church world. I wanted my independence and desired a taste of worldly excitement. I felt such a void in my life, and during that time, church was not fulfilling all my human appetite and natural instincts. Back in those days, my mother, and the church we were affiliated with did not deal with significant life issues relating to womanhood, sex, courtship, or dating. Within our community children learned and lived by the framework of our parents' religious beliefs. By this time, I was very resentful and disagreeable with my mom for her sternness.

I had a cousin named Linda whom I loved like a sister, and she was my partying partner. When she passed away, I was devastated. She was a couple of years older than me, and we would go to the clubs on the military base every weekend to party. Mother allowed us to go out if we were in the house by curfew. I resented that curfew because that was the time when all the excitement really started. When it was too late to go home, we would simply stay out. By this time, my drinking was increasing, and I experienced episodes of intoxication. Eventually, I began dating military guys. There was a soldier named Gary whom I met while partying at the club and hanging out with friends. He was very funny and kept us laughing. He impressed me even though he was shy and low-key. I noticed he kept watching me during our interaction with friends. I noticed Gary spending quite of bit of money, and he had a nice red car. He was always nice and respectful toward me, something I did not get from the other guys. Gary really enjoyed bowling and was good at it, so bowling became another one of my social outlets. I would invite my sisters and church friends to go with us to the bowling alley. I began to enjoy Gary's company;

CHAPTER 2

Married for the Wrong Reasons

ONE DAY GARY CAME TO MY MOM'S HOUSE TO TELL ME THAT HE RECEIVED orders for deployment to Vietnam for a couple of years. I do not remember how the conversation came up, but we discussed getting married. All I saw were dollar signs and security. We told my mom, and she kept asking us, "Are y'all sure?" He said yes. I knew I was not ready for marriage because I still enjoyed my freedom and going to the club. The option to marry triggered a greater freedom: an escape from my mother's house rules. Therefore, I persuaded him that I loved him and was ready for marriage.

We left town and traveled to Washington, DC. Gary took me to this expensive jewelry store located in the city to purchase wedding rings. They were beautiful, glittered so bright, and were expensive. He reserved a hotel room for an overnight stay after we finished shopping. I had never received this level of romance from a man. I loved and enjoyed the attention he gave me, and I did not have to compromise my body. I wondered how this man could be willing to take me as his wife knowing my history. I really wondered how this man could trust me to be faithful while stationed in Vietnam. I convinced myself this was my chance to escape into a world of independence and security. We had a special dinner date in a fabulous restaurant within the hotel. That night was unforgettable with laughter and enjoying our time together. We continued to talk about getting married and making wedding plans.

We returned to my hometown the next day and informed my parents of our plans. Mom kept asking both of us, "Are y'all sure? Are you ready for this?" I answered yes, and Gary followed with a very respectful "Yes, ma'am." After meeting with my parents, I wanted to go to the club so badly, but Gary wanted to go bowling, so we invited friends to go bowling with us on the military base. The following week, we went to South Carolina to get married on a Friday and returned to my parents' house. My parents, friends, and family congratulated us, and we stayed at my parents' house that night. Mom gave us one of the bedrooms to spend our wedding night at her house. Believe me, I had a hidden agenda for later that night, and it did not include my husband. On our wedding night, I convinced Gary to allow me to drive his car to the club without him. I snuck out of the house, trying not to wake my parents. It was around the time when the club was just beginning to rock. Here I was, just married earlier that day, but I left my husband in bed to go out to party with other guys. This man loved me and simply wanted to make me happy. Sin had yoked me up, so I lived my life without a decent conscience. This action spoke to my state of mind at the time. Gary was the kindest man anyone could want for a husband. I do not know what I was looking for or running away from during this time because I had the potential of having it all with Gary. The truth was I did not love myself! It was obvious that I was not ready to settle down, be faithful to my husband, and be committed to marriage. Gary, being the gentleman he was, said "OKAY."

My mother did not know I had left out until the next morning. Mom asked Gary, "Where is Christine?"

He replied, "I don't know, but she went to the club last night."

Mom questioned him, "You let Christine go out on your wedding night, and you don't know where she is?"

"Yes, ma'am," he replied. When I came in, Mom was upset with me, and she started fussing, but Gary did not say anything. I was remorseful about staying out all night, leaving my husband on a celebratory night. Gary did not deserve that, especially on our wedding night. I apologized to him and reassured him I was faithful to him that night.

Before his deployment, Gary made sure that I obtained a military ID card and started all the paperwork for me to receive military benefits and privileges. He was leaving his car with me so I would have transportation. Gary and I were still living with my parents, and I spent all my time with him. On the day he left for deployment, it made me sad and afraid because he was going to war. I did consider the possibilities of him not returning to me, but I rejected those thoughts. As I cried, he embraced me, reassuring that everything was going to be all right.

Once he arrived and settled on base in Vietnam, he called to let me know they had made it safely. I cannot remember how long I waited before I started frequenting the clubs again, but it was not long. Now I had my own transportation and money, and I was in control of my own life. I was everywhere except where I was supposed to have been as a faithful wife to my husband. After the initial call, we communicated by mail for a couple of weeks. After a couple of months of his deployment to Vietnam, Gary has attempted to contact me, but I was doing my own thing. I was traveling out of town and being unfaithful. I was everywhere but at home, and not even my parents knew my whereabouts. I would be away from home for a couple of weeks at a time. Even when I returned home, I was still partying hard and staying out all night. I was getting my allotment check every month from Gary's military pay, but I wasted it living a wild and unsettled lifestyle. My correspondence with Gary decreased significantly, and I would miss his phone calls. When I returned home, my parents would tell me, "You missed Gary's call again." My mother was not pleased with how I was neglecting my marriage and living my life. Since Gary's departure, I had spoken to him only twice, and one of those calls was his initial call after being based in Vietnam. My mother was right: I was neglecting my marriage vows.

One night upon leaving the club intoxicated, I wrecked Gary's car. I drove it into a ditch. Gary took pride in his car, so I knew this might be his breaking point. Gary had contacted the Red Cross to assist in finding my location, because it had been two months since he had heard from me. The Red Cross contacted my parents, attempting to get information about my whereabouts. They left a number for me to return the call, and I did. The Red Cross arranged a day and time to connect me with Gary by phone from his base in Vietnam. I was not looking forward to confessing my unfaithfulness and telling him about wrecking his car. When we did connect by phone, I apologized to him for my lack of communication and told him I had wrecked his car. I felt so bad and remorseful because my husband deserved better. He made it known that he was disappointed and upset about his car. He asked me, "Where is my car now?" I told him that I parked it in my parents' yard. I knew by the tone of his voice my marriage might be in jeopardy. I was truly sorrowful for breaking my husband's heart because he had been good to me. Gary never claimed to be a Christian, but he was a gentleman, a man of integrity, a decent individual, and he was a good husband. I was the problem because of my sinful nature. I acknowledged my lack of consideration of what my husband had to face while at war in Vietnam, in addition to worrying about his unfaithful wife. Everything about my life and my concerns were selfish: I feared losing all my military benefits and my marriage. I had to admit to myself when I married Gary, I was not in love with him. I was in love with the idea of being married. I did not even love myself, and I struggled inwardly with self-worth. At the end of our phone conversation, Gary had little to say, but I attempted to reassure him that I loved him. Mom became even more displeased with me, because she knew I was about to forfeit a good thing with Gary.

I continued to stay at my parents' house, trying to get myself together, but the strongholds of sin had me yoked up. I continued partying at clubs and tried to comply with Mom's curfew or mom would lock me out of the house. There were times I stayed out all night and returned home the next day. Gary, being who he was, continued to support me financially. I was not depending on my parents to take care of me, so their opinions did not change my mind or behaviors.

CHAPTER 3

Walking in the Dark

As TIME PROGRESSED, MY CIRCLE OF ASSOCIATES BECAME MORE TOXIC, which caused me to experience circumstances I never could have imagined. Peer pressure had overpowered my will to do what I knew would be in my best interests. I was losing touch of any convictions that were a part of my foundational teachings. This church girl had gone astray and gone wild, indulging in all kinds of sins: fornication, alcohol, drug abuse, and illicit behavior. I connected myself with procurers, "ladies of the night," drug traffickers, drug users, and those who had committed criminal crimes. All these sinful acts distorted my thinking and perception, which gave me a false sense of acceptance. I was delusional about the consequences of living such a corrupted lifestyle. The reality was, I had lost control over my life, and was enslave by demonic forces. What was more terrifying about my lifestyle was that I convinced myself it was passable. The ladies of the night accepted me and educated me to the street games, and they influenced me to participate in illegal activities.

One night I went to a popular location that was known for all illicit activities. There were ladies of the night everywhere and those seeking to make fast money through illegal activities. There were night clubs up and down the street with entertainment of exotic dancers. The police drove up and down the road, patrolling for any potential crimes. The movement of the fast life, getting attention from different guys, and the bright lights were captivating and inviting, so I embraced the street game. I started walking the streets with the ladies of the night.

My illicit behaviors had progressed to stealing (larceny), working as a lady of the night, abusing illicit drugs, and being an accessory to robbery. Being a lady of the night was a total makeover from my identity which included wearing revealing and provocative clothing, colorful wigs, heavy makeup, and high-heeled shoes. Now I was entertaining strangers for money. There were times I questioned myself, "How did I get here? Where have my innocence and that chosen child gone?" I was too embarrassed to return home because of guilt and shame. My mother had a powerful spirit of discernment, and I knew she would have sensed through the spirit of every unclean spirit attached to me. I never would have dreamed in a million years I would have stooped so low, performing forbidden sins after having the teaching and values she had instilled in me. The guilt and shame were overwhelming because the seed of righteousness remained within me. The consciousness of my spirit made me restless. I cannot count the many nights I cried myself to sleep wanting out of this bondage.

My mom had not seen me in a couple of months. I heard that Mom was inform by neighbors of my lifestyle and drug use. One night I was walking in an area I frequented, not knowing that my mom would be out that night looking for me. It was on a Thursday night. My mother would normally be in church on Thursday night for prayer meeting services until 10:00 p.m. As I was walking, I heard someone calling out my name. "Chris!" It sounded like the voice of my mom. It was my mom! When I looked across the street toward where the sound was coming from, I saw her driving by and slowly yelling my name, "Chris! Chris!" I dashed inside a club to hide from her, knowing she would never come inside a club. Ladies were passing by, and I asked them to watch out for me and to let me know when my mom was no longer in sight. I stayed in the club for about fifteen minutes because I could not face my mom, especially wearing a revealing seductive outfit. Now I felt terrible, even more shameful, and guilty, because she knew the truth about her daughter. I could imagine the pain and tears that were running down her face as she drove back home. Knowing my mother, after witnessing me walking the streets, she returned home to pray for my salvation and safety. I knew my parents were worried about me, but I was in too deep to get out. My mother always kept her children in prayer and constantly pleaded the blood of Jesus Christ over our lives.

My life started spiraling downhill because of my drug abuse and illegal behaviors. I was not eating properly, and I was getting little sleep because I would go out at night to walk the streets until daybreak. I often resided where there were drug activities. I know it was my mother's prayers covering me from potential danger, because danger was all around me, but God's grace and mercy kept me protected.

I became acquainted with a man named Slim, he just got out of prison a couple of weeks prior to meeting him. Slim was his nickname on the streets because he stood about six feet, six inches. He had a thin body, light brown complexion, a short beard, and had a muscular build. The day we met, I was infatuate with his looks, kindness, and conversation. I did not ask him why he was in prison and just assumed it was drug related. We departed on a positive note, and I could tell he was interested in developing an intimate relationship with me. The second time I met him, he boldly said to me, "I want you to be my lady," and he told me how fine I was.

As I turned to walk away, he reached out to touch my hands and started flirting with me. I melted, grinned from ear to ear, and said, "Thank you!" I agreed to become his lady. I continued drinking, smoking marijuana, and I began snorting heroin. I minimized the seriousness of my drug problem because I was not injecting heroin. I was streetwalking to get money to buy drugs, and I woke up every morning planning my next drug use. I was living from house to house with associates who had my common interests: using drugs and making money. Walking the streets at night exposed me to unexpected danger because I never knew whose car I was jumping into; there was always the risk of putting my life in danger by entertaining strangers.

I was a victim of rape, beaten, and left in unfamiliar and isolated places by the men I was entertaining. One would think the fear and potential near-death encounters would have convinced me to return home. I had a loving family waiting for me to return. I did not have to live on the street and expose myself to this abuse. This illicit involvement enslaved and imprisoned me from just living a normal and happy life. I felt helpless and powerless.

Slim and I pursued our relationship and started using drugs together. One night, Slim and I decided to take intravenous heroin. Slim said, "This is the first time I've shot up heroin." That day was the first time I allowed peer pressure to persuade me to inject heroin. Immediately I felt a rush that went straight to my brain, and I became violently sick. I started vomiting all over the place. I could hardly hold up my head, which felt like it was spinning. My vision was blurry, and I was nodding in and out to the point that I almost fell out of the chair. I thought I was going to die from this high because of the side effects, but I survived. That was the beginning of my journey as an intravenous heroin user. I became even more free-spirited, indulging more in all kinds of illegal behaviors, and my drug use increased. I started going back to the clubs, mostly to clubs on the military base.

Eventually, Slim started spending more nights with me wherever we laid our heads. He did not pressure me to give him money, but there was a nonverbal agreement that we shared what I had. We would share my income to get high or to meet basic needs. As time passed, I later found out that Slim was known for committing robberies. I reckoned that was why he had been in prison. He did his thing to get money, and I did my thing. He had a reputation on the streets that was very colorful, and he was not one to cross or challenge; people on the streets called him Shotgun.

The people we lived with did their thing, but when the night was over, we all came home with money to get high or intoxicated. I started developing stronger feelings for Slim, but I was still wild and enjoyed clubbing, dancing, and drinking. I was very promiscuous. Slim started getting more possessive, argumentative, and controlling, demanding I engage in illicit behaviors to get money. I was still getting my allotment check from my husband, but I wasted it getting high and on riotous living. I was getting tired of walking the streets all night long just to get money to get high. Slim and I had an intense argument about money that resulted in a bad breakup. Slim stayed away for weeks, and I was relieved because I was afraid of his rage. I heard that he was increasingly robbing stores. Because it had been a while since I had seen Slim, I freed myself from any obligations to him. I went out to party more at the club. I was participating in dancing contests and partying hard with my friends. Slim and I had broken up, so I felt free to do my thing without him controlling my every move. I was spending more time walking the streets with the ladies of the night and entertaining strangers for money.

One night, while walking the streets, my dad was walking through town, heading toward the corner I would walk during the night. He was walking home because his car had broken down. That route was the nearest route he could take to get home. I ran to hide behind a building until he passed by. I wanted to also make sure no one solicited my dad. As I observed Dad passing by, he walked quickly and looked straight ahead. Seeing Dad reminded me of my loving family I had forsaken. Even more guilt, shame, and remorse gripped my heart. I was walking the streets more, being visible, and people from my home church would see me. I knew people were judging me harshly for what I was doing and for my seductive outfits. I heard people would make a mockery of my mother being a preacher while her daughter was a lady of the night. I had no doubt that my mother was consistently praying and fasting for me. Mom's prayers were driving back demonic forces that intended to destroy my life. I could feel her prayers because that spiritual connection remained in me. I started feeling conscientious about what I was doing but did not have the power to break away or the will to change my behaviors.

CHAPTER 4

Too Deep to Get Out

MY CLOSEST FACE-OFF WITH DEATH SINCE LEAVING HOME WAS AN encounter with Slim. Slim thought I was seeing someone else and heard about me partying with other guys. He was in a rage as he walked upstairs pointing a sawed-off shotgun at my face. Fear overcame me, and I yelled out, crying, and begging him, "Slim, please don't!" I looked at the rage in his eyes and the anger on his face as he used profane and degrading language, accusing me of playing him. I denied his accusations and apologized. I was crying hysterically as he stared at me. I stood there in shock, scared to move, with tears running down my face. I apologized for hurting him. Nobody but God turned a potential tragedy around and blocked the devil's plan to bring harm or kill me that day. I believed at that moment, God dispatched His warring angels to drive back the spirit of death and lower that sawed-off shotgun in his hands. Hallelujah! Glory to God! It was then that I realized why people called him Shotgun!

That was one of the closest encounters of facing death I had experienced since leaving home. I was too terrified to leave his presence, so I attempted to resolve our differences and reconcile our relationship. We reunited, but the message was clear: my life was at risk if I tried to leave him. Slim moved back in with me a couple of months later, I started having morning sickness. Oh my! I was pregnant! Slim was so excited because this would be his first child. He became more concerned about me and was less violent. He started checking on me more frequently to make sure I was doing okay. In fact, Slim became a little more protective of me because of my pregnancy. Slim did not want me to go out, and therefore I stayed off the streets for a little while. Slim was committing robberies in surrounding areas. I heard over the news of a store robbery, but the suspects got away. I heard increasingly about robberies on the news. Slim would come upstairs to our bedroom with packs of cigarettes, extra money, money bags, and his sawed-off shotgun. I knew it was Slim committing these crimes, but I pretended I was ignorant to what was going on because I feared him.

During this time, I was feeling the intensity of my mom's prayers. I could not sleep or rest at night. I had a fervent desire to visit with my family and be in the presence of my mom. I had resistance about going home because my shame and guilt were so overwhelming. I asked myself, "How can I return back home to face my mom knowing she knows what I am doing?" The demonic forces really had control over my mind and will. I could feel the pulling of my mom's prayers arresting my will to come home. During my adolescence, I remembered seeing and hearing demonic forces coming subject under the power of my mom's prayers. I witness the supernatural power in operation through her prayers and the power of God operating in our church. I had not made any contact with my family or my husband for a while. As I reflect on this time of my life, the devil used the spirit of condemnation to keep me away from my family. The devil had me feeling hopeless and unlovable. The devil's intent was to prohibit me from reaching my kingdom destiny, and keep me disconnected from my family, especially my mother. I often recalled the words my mother spoke over my life: "You are chosen! God is going to use you!" I was falling deeper and deeper in sin and in a dark, bottomless pit.

CHAPTER 5

The Power of My Mother's Prayers

I REMEMBER THE DAY I DECIDED TO RETURN HOME. I SIMPLY WANTED TO let mom know I was still alive and well. I knew I was not looking well because of weight loss and lack of sleep. I walked about eight miles to get to my parents' house because I had no means of transportation. My siblings were outside playing, and Dad was walking onto the front porch. I felt so unworthy to go inside the house, so I sat on the porch with my eyes focused on the ground in shame. I heard Dad call out to Mom with much excitement, "Ruth! Ruth! Christine is home!"

My sister said, "Mom has locked herself in the bathroom, praying and crying out for God to send you home." They told me that Mom had been on a twelve-day fast (no food, just eating ice), praying and crying out for my protection and return home. That day, it was the power of prayer that drew me back home. Dad said to me, "Ruth has been sick from not eating."

When Mom finally came out of the bathroom onto the porch, she ran toward me with tears running down her face and embraced me tightly. She said, "Oh, Chris, I'm glad to see you! I had dreams of you in a ditch, dead!" She did not know a couple of months before, I had experienced a face-to-face near-death experience. I recalled that loaded sawed-off shotgun Slim had pointed to my head. Now, I know this incident happened during the time my mom was in consecration, travailing and praying continuously for me. Even as I am writing and reflecting on the abundant goodness of God, with His grace and mercies shown toward me, tears fill my eyes. I feel a burst of gratitude and joy right now because I could have died, and my soul would have been in hell.

Mom walked me into the house and loved on me compassionately, hugging and crying while holding me in her arms. I know my appearance was unkempt, and I looked unhealthy. She never mentioned how I looked and simply praised God that I was home. She repeatedly said, "I am glad you came home." She kept asking me, "How are you doing?" As she was talking, she told me that Gary, my husband, was trying to contact me. I could not call him back because he was still in Vietnam. I knew Mom and Dad thought I was back home for good, but I could not stay even if I wanted to. I did not want to put them at risk due to any problems with Slim. I spent time with the family and made amends with my parents for what I had done. I stayed with them a couple of days to get rest and have peace of mind.

Unexpectedly, Slim showed up to my parents' house looking for me. Someone had directed him to where my parents lived. He showed up requesting I return with him. He was upset because I had left the apartment without telling him where I was going. I did not want Slim to have any contact with my family. While I visited with my mom, I did not say anything about my pregnancy because I did not want to add to the burdens of her heart concerning me.

I returned with Slim to the same insane and vicious cycle, using drugs and tolerating the abuse. I was back on the streets engaging in illicit behavior, stealing, and running and hiding from the police. I knew I was a couple of months pregnant, but I continued to use heroin and walk the streets because I needed money to take care of my basic needs and support my addiction. I continued to lose weight because I was not eating properly. I had not received any prenatal care, neglecting not only me but also my unborn baby. The apartment where I was residing had become known for selling drugs and other illegal activities. I got the word that the house was under surveillance by undercover detectives. I tried to be more cautious with my illegal involvement. One night while walking the streets, I solicited an undercover police officer. He pulled out his badge, cuffed my hands, and put me into the police car. That was my first charge for solicitation. They released me on bond that night from jail. All I could think of at the time was the possibility of my husband finding out I was walking the streets as a lady of the night.

Demonic forces had their strongholds wrapped around my mind, and I was bound up mentally, emotionally, and spiritually. My life had become progressively worse, and I had been nothing but unfaithful to my husband. Dad contacted me to inform me that Gary had a certified document at the house through the Red Cross requesting my whereabouts again. My parents had knowledge of my whereabouts because I was residing in the same neighborhood of my late aunt Rena. My dad would visit her sometimes to try to get information about me or to leave messages.

During my experiences on the streets, it was extremely dangerous, and I experienced countless near-death encounters. The only reason I escaped to tell my story is because of the fervent, effectual prayers of the righteous.

I knew it was time for me to come off the streets for a while because of morning sickness and neglecting my health. I had a solicitation charge, my health was declining, and my body was growing weaker from walking the streets and doing drugs. My life was going down the drain! I felt like I was at the lowest of low, and the best way I can describe the state of my life is a human living in a hog pen. My thinking and judgment were so impaired. I continued to inject heroin while pregnant and failed to seek prenatal care. I continued to get high to escape the pain and misery of my life. I did not want my baby to have any deformities or addicted, but I knew that was a consequence of my continuous drug use. The insanity of my thinking was so obvious. I became so acclimated with the conditions I was living in. I knew I had to prepare for motherhood, so I decided I was going to seek employment to avoid getting another criminal charge. I still had access to drugs where I was living. I finally was employed as a waiter at a popular soul food restaurant. This job took me off the streets for a little while.

Slim continued committing robberies. He would keep information about his criminal activities from me. He never shared with me what he planned to do or what he did. I would see evidence of money and substantial amounts of cigarette packs, and I knew he had that sawed-off shotgun. One night while I was working, a friend came into the restaurant to tell me Slim had sustained a gunshot in his leg while robbing a store. I told my boss I had a family emergency and had to leave immediately. I arrived at our apartment, where Slim was waiting for me. He needed medical assistance but feared going to the emergency room because of the risk of investigation and being arrested. When I ran upstairs, he was on the bed bleeding. He was in excruciating pain with a large hole in his leg.

He had wrapped a towel around his leg, trying to slow down the bleeding. I was so nervous and scared because I had never experienced anything like this before, not to mention attending to a gunshot wound that could lead to him bleeding out. Slim asked me to help him slow down the bleeding by applying pressure. He said, "Get the peroxide antiseptic and pour some in the wound. Wrap it with a towel and put pressure on it."

I was nervous. Slim became irritated with my hesitation and started yelling at me to just do it. He hollered so loud until I was shaking and paralyzed with fear. Later, Slim went to another location for further medical attention and to hide from the police. I had to avoid being around him for a while so I would not be an accessory to his crime. I later heard about the robbery on the news. The suspects murdered the store owner during the robbery, and one suspect escaped with a gunshot wound. I almost collapsed on the floor because I knew of the victim. He was the kindest man one could have met, and I shopped at this store often. I was so angry with Slim for committing this senseless act against a very respectable, loving, and caring individual in the community. Slim stayed away from the apartment, and I made no efforts to locate him. I was so afraid of this man to the point that I did whatever he told me to do. I knew not to ask him what had happened the night he sustained a gunshot injury to his leg. I felt like the less I knew, the safer I would be from any crimes related to the murder. Slim became a suspect, and the police began searching and watching our apartment and every move. My eyes were truly open to the reality that my life and freedom might be in danger.

I returned to my parents' house to get away from our associates at that time and to avoid the possibility of the investigators arresting or questioning me. Mom was so glad I returned home but she did not know the danger I was facing. She did not know that the man I was pregnant by was a murderer. I heard people within the community expressing anger about the killing. The victim was one respected and loved for his kindness shown toward his customers. I eventually had to tell mom and dad about what I had heard and what I knew about the killing, and about the threat on my life. I was so terrified for my own life! I did not want to endanger my family with another unexpected visit from Slim. My mom, being a praying woman and a faith walker, said to me, "God isn't going to let that man hurt you, and you are covered by the blood of Jesus Christ!" Again,

Mom's anointed words were soothing and settled my spirit, but I was still battling with the fear of Slim finding me.

Gary continued to stay in contact with my family by mail or calling when he could. When I came to my parents' house, a certified legal document was waiting for me from an attorney appointed by my husband. Gary had filed for a divorce on grounds of abandonment or something to that effect. I knew it was justifiable, but I did not want a divorce because the military benefits were my security. We had been married a little over a year, and I was about to be divorced. I was married on paper but never at heart. I knew for sure Gary was a faithful and a good husband, but I was an adulterer because of sin. He was good to both my family and me. He provided money to my parents to resolve financial challenges; therefore, I was not surprised by the cohesive bond between him and my family. One day while at my parents' house, Gary unexpectedly showed up on an emergency leave. He came to get his car that I had wrecked and to tell me that he had filed for divorce. I tried to plead with him and manipulate him to be intimate with me, because I did not want to lose him and the military benefits. I was already pregnant by Slim, but my plan was to pretend I had gotten pregnant by Gary. Gary refused, but he was calm and respectful toward me. Mom was very distraught and apologetic to Gary for what I had done to him. I watched Gary as he drove away with so much disappointment and hurt on his face. There were no words I could say to reconcile our marriage.

There was a lengthy process before we could be officially divorced, so I was able to hold on to my military benefits a little longer. My bad choices were catching up with me, and now I had to deal with the consequences. My world was crumbling, and I was spiraling downward at an accelerated rate. My mom continued to pray, fast, and cry out on my behalf. When mom would see me, she often reminded me of who I was in the kingdom of God, "God's chosen child," and she would say, "God has His hand on you." I remember Mom telling me how everyone was expressing concern about her personal health, because mom was worrying about me and my welfare. She would tell me how people would speak of me in a judgmental tone. Mom said her response was, "When you all see Christine, you might see a person addicted to drugs and a lady of the night, but she continued to confess of my salvation. I see my daughter being born again!" Mom kept speaking life over me. She would prophesy my destiny, canceling out the reports of the devil and proclaiming what God called me, "a chosen child." Even during the darkest and lowest times of my life, she continued to prophesy, "Chris, you are chosen by God!"

I remembered the house prayer meetings Mom would have at home every Monday at noon, and the shut-ins interceding for unsaved souls. Mom had prayer early in the morning, as well as noonday prayer at church or at home. Her house rules required everyone in her house to bow in prayer when she called for family prayer. Being in Mom's presence brought calmness to my fears. I remained separated and detached from my old friends for a while. I avoided all association with Slim or anyone connected with him. I did not want to be a suspect or accessory to a murder crime after the fact. I did not want anyone to put my family at risk. I laid down and woke up with intense fear of this man. It had been almost two weeks since I had used any drugs, and I was having withdrawal symptoms, but I endured the discomfort. I stayed confined at home with my parents.

One afternoon when I was in the kitchen alone, I heard a noise at the back door, and someone rushed in and said, "Boo!" I ran out of the house hollering and crying. I was so frightened to the point that I did not wait to see anyone, but I ran to where my mom was, visiting one of the church mothers who lived nearby; we called her Momma Lottie. Dad was at work, and my siblings were outside playing. Mom came running out the house toward me. "What's wrong with you, Chris?" I responded with a trembling voice and tears running down my face, "Somebody broke into the back door!" Mom walked me back to the house to see what was going on. People were outside asking what was wrong. Mom stepped into her house boldly, and there stood my brother Jeffery. Mom asked Jeff what had happened. Jeff replied, "That was me playing and trying to scare Christine." I was relieved when my brother confessed it was him, but I was still upset.

Mom was also upset with Jeff and punished him. I heard Mom saying to Jeff as she was punishing him, "Don't you ever do that again to that girl!" I felt sorry for Jeff because I knew he did not know his joke was going to upset me to that degree. I did not attend church with Mom while staying with her, but I was in the midst during prayer time at home. Regardless of my sinful ways, I could still feel the love and presence of God when Mom prayed. Tears would run down my face, but I was not ready to totally surrender because I was too deep in this risky and unpredictable lifestyle. I continue to lay low, hiding from Slim in fear and feeling discontentment of heart. My pregnancy was noticeable, and I still had not seen a doctor. Mom continued to show love and expressed concerns about my health.

After a couple of weeks at my parents' house, I decided to relocate to New York to distance myself from Slim and potentially from the police. After a month of residing in New York, I received a phone call informing me that the police had arrested Slim. I was so relieved after hearing of his confinement. After staying in New York for a brief time, I relocated to New Jersey to live with one of my mother's sisters, Aunt Lena. While living with her I decided to arrange for an appointment to see a doctor for prenatal care. The doctor gave me a good report about my pregnancy. The doctor prescribed prenatal care vitamins and other medicines. The doctor said my baby's heartbeat was good, and his body size looked normal from the ultrasound. I was so grateful but knew it was because of the goodness of God and my mother's prayers. I stayed in New Jersey until Slim received his sentence to prison.

While in New Jersey I connected with other drug users and returned to sporadically injecting heroin. I slowed down my activities in the street when I was in my third trimester. Family members called to tell me that Slim received 120 years in prison for felony crimes which included two murders. His crimes and sentencing were in the local newspaper. During the trial, he had the support only of his mother. His father was deceased, and Slim was an only child. His mother died a couple of years after his confinement.

After he went to prison, I returned to my parents' house to give birth to my son. My baby, Travis Lavon Byndon, was born March 6, 1972, without any birth defects or any special needs. There was no trace of drugs in either Travis's or my system, nobody but God intervened on my behalf. I knew it was only by the grace of God because I was still using drugs. Again, that was a testament to God's goodness and my mother's prayers. Travis, or Von as I called him, was born at a military hospital. I still had my military benefits under my husband's name even though he was in the process of divorcing me. I was nineteen years old when I birthed Travis. A couple of months after birthing Travis, I received my divorce papers and the checks ceased.

When I looked in Travis's precious little face, all I could see was his father, Slim. He resembled his father so much. My thoughts centered on how I was going to protect him from his father, and how would I tell him that his father was in prison for murder. I brought Von home with me to my parents' home, where I was residing. When my mother laid eyes on her first grandson, the love and joy she expressed as she held him close to her chest was priceless. As I watched Mom's Interaction with Von, I knew he had made a special imprint in her heart forever.

For a couple of months, I was able to take care of my son with the financial assistance from my parents. I applied for welfare assistance and was approve for Medicaid and Food Stamps. I noticed that Von knew the difference between his grandma's arms and mine. Almost immediately when Mom picked him up, he would stop crying. Every time Von would cry or I would turn my head, my mom was picking him up or rocking him. She became attached to Von and spoiled him. If I had to go out to manage business, Mom always wanted Von to remain with her. I eventually reconnected with old friends and my cousin Linda, who was my partying partner. Mom would allow my cousin and me to go out if we were back by midnight. I knew her house rules and had no problem complying because I had a son to consider. I wanted to demonstrate a sense of parental responsibility. I convinced myself that I could reconnect with my old friends while having no intention of returning to street life or using drugs. I was free from any threats of Slim, but I was not free from my demons.

At the time, I thought I was strong enough to resist the temptation and entanglement of the same vicious cycle of using drugs, illicit behavior, and criminal activities. I made a poor judgment call when I reconnected with old associates. They were doing the same things, abusing drugs, and engaging in criminal activities. I had been clean now for a couple of months, but after reconnecting with them, my desire to use drugs increased. Eventually, I was back on that insane merry-go-around. I started going out more, but I returned home every night to my baby. I knew hanging out late at night would not be a continuous and permissible routine while living at my parents' house. I did not want to disrespect Mom's house rule or pour salt into the open wounds of her heart that I caused. My mom had made so many countless sacrifices for me. Neither did I want to expose my son to any danger and my addictive behaviors. When I would go out to party, I always left my son with mom.

One day I decided to apply for low-income Housing Urban Development (HUD) housing for my son and me to have our own residence. HUD approved me for housing within a couple of months, and I moved into my own apartment behind my parents' house. Living close to Mom would allow her to see her grandchild when she desired, and it was convenient for me if I needed a babysitter. I was so excited about having my own place, and I convinced myself that things would be different, especially because I was a mother. Even though I relapsed, I would not allow myself to overindulge. My mom really did not want me to leave her house, especially with Von, but she was more willing to accept it, because the apartment was directly behind her. I was less than five minutes away.

After living in my own apartment for about three months, Linda and I started going out more and partying with guys from my apartment complex. Even though I was near my parents' house, my parents respected my space. I met a guy named James who expressed attraction toward me. He participated in a business that generated fast money through illicit activities. I watched as he pulled out a large bundle of folded bills. I was impressed by the money, and he was a big spender. He really treated me special and took a liking to my son. He would stop by often to my apartment to give me money and bring items for Von. I was leaving Von with Mom more often and spending more time at James's house. I found myself back on the streets walking in the night and doing more drugs. James became my man and my drug supplier and did not object to my drug use. My parents had no idea I had returned to walking the streets and doing drugs; Mom thought Linda and I were simply partying at the clubs. In addition to walking the streets, I started pushing drugs for James.

I eventually introduced James to Mom, and he impressed her with his charm. He had his own house and car and was financially secure, even though it was money from illegal activities. When Mom's refrigerator stopped working, James decided to replace it. That impressed her. He was very respectful and kind toward her. He even reassured her that he loved me and was going to take care of me. He accepted Von and did not mind having him over to his house, but Mom was not going to let her grandson be gone for long. My time spent at James' house was more than the time spent with Von. His house was a gathering place for our friends to come over to socialize, mostly for playing cards and drinking. I continued to maintain my apartment to keep my housing under the HUD program and my welfare benefits. I also maintained the residence as a safe place for my son and me. The more I stayed around this man, the more I fell for him. It was because he gave me a false sense of security having money and drugs available.

Things were getting progressively worse for me because of my increased drug usage. I spent less time with my son, but I knew he was safe with Mom. I was missing time with him and those precious moments of bonding and nurturing my baby boy. I did not realize at the time that James might have a drinking problem. The evidence was obvious as I witnessed his continuous drinking early in the mornings and throughout the day. His behaviors began to change, and he became very possessive, controlling, and abusive. The relationship issues with James were no different from what I had experienced with other procurers. Each time I was in a low place, in a high-risk situation, or in a crisis, I could feel the prayers of my mom. I can testify of the manifested power of my mother's prayers, because I was a beneficiary throughout my childhood. Those moments planted seeds of faith in the power of God. I am sure my dad was praying for me too. I forgot to mention that my dad eventually gave his life to God during one of my mom's house prayer meetings. My dad never turned his back on me, even after having knowledge of my drug uses. He was always there to support me when I needed his assistance. I thank God that my parents always welcome me home no matter what I did.

One day while I visited my son at my parents' home, Gary showed up unexpectedly. I could not hide the shame and guilt I felt when I looked into his eyes. I reflected on my unfaithfulness in our marriage, and again I was apologetic. Being the kindhearted man that he was, he was respectful toward me during our interaction. He told me that he had heard about me on the streets and knew everything I was doing. I could not deny it! I tried to find out where he had received his information, and we had small talk. After making amends and processing our feelings, Gary and I had an intimate moment. After spending time together, he visited with the family for a moment. Gary had a tight bond with my family and would visit often despite our failed marriage. I was still with James and still engaging in illicit activities. Mom expressed concerns with me for not spending more time Von but agreed to care for him while I was away.

One night while at James's house, I heard his doorbell ring. I was in the back bedroom injecting heroin. James answered the door. I did not check to see who it was because people were in and out all the time. I was so high from using heroin that I was not concerned and was not attentive to who came in. Shortly, I heard a gunshot fired. James said panicky, "I been shot!" James came into the bedroom where I was sitting; he was limping and bleeding from a gunshot wound to his leg. There were two guys in disguise following behind him armed with guns. One guy pointed a gun in his back and the other intruder pointed a gun at me. They ordered us to get into the bathroom and do not make a sound. We remained there for about five minutes. We finally heard the guys running out and slamming the door. My high had left me, and reality kicked in that my life might be at risk. We sat in the bathroom for about five minutes, and then James said, "Let's get out of here before they come back in and kill us!" We were able to get out of the bathroom and into the car, and we drove away. As we were driving around the corner, we were able to see a car driving toward James's house. We assumed it was the men returning to the house to kill us. James went to the emergency room for medical care, and he reported the robbery. We were not able to identify the intruders because they had their faces covered. I was sure he was not going to report what had happened because drugs were involved. Again, God allowed me to escape death. Afterwards, I found out there was a contract on James's life. I was convinced that James might have serious issues with sources within his circle. I thank God for the covering of protection through the prayers of Mom.

I went back to my apartment for safety. I stayed off the streets and decreased my drug use for a couple of months. I was informed that an anonymous individual reported my illicit activities to the Housing Authority. Someone reported I was performing illegal activities at my apartment. HUD evicted me from that apartment, and I lost all benefits under HUD. I lost funding and now had to pay rent out of pocket. The community I moved in was in a high-risk community for crimes, but the rent was affordable. My new location was much farther away from my parents' home. Mom was unable to see Von every day as normal, so she would stop by often to get him to spend nights with her. She expressed concern about the neighbor and individuals coming in and out of my trailer. Mom knew my living status was not healthy for her grandson, so to put her mind at ease, she took him to her house. Von made it known to me that he preferred being with his grandmother rather than with me, he would cry for her when she visited. He was one years old, walking, and able to say a couple of words.

As time progressed, I began to feel sick in the mornings, nauseous, vomiting and I was gaining weight. It was shocking to find out I was pregnant again. I thought this baby was James, and he did too. I finally visited the doctor and found out that I was pregnant with a baby girl. I was shocked and concerned about my baby's health because I was still using drugs. When I gave birth to my baby girl, she was so beautiful that I did not believe she was my baby. It was obvious she was not James's baby. She was a very light-skinned baby with a head full of beautiful, slick black hair going down her neck. She had none of James's features. Then, I recalled the intimate moment Gary and I had. I called him to tell him that he has a daughter. He was in disbelief and made plans to see her. I was so thankful to God because there was no deformity, and she appeared healthy. There was no trace of drugs in her or my system. When the nurse brought her into my room, I said to her, "I think you gave me the wrong baby!" I remember thinking she was too pretty to be my baby. I named her Teresa, but we called her Tee for short.

When Gary saw Teresa, he immediately bonded with her and called her his little girl. Tee had his features. Tee did not have to worry about anything as long as Gary was around and that was often. He never missed a Christmas or birthday when it came to celebrating her. Von and Tee were a year apart. There was times Gary would take Tee to Ohio to spend time with his family, and they embraced and loved her. When she was in her adolescence, I allowed Tee to spend the summer with her dad in New Mexico. Even though Gary knew I was still out on the streets and doing drugs, he stepped in, fulfilling parental obligations in my stead, and providing for both Von and Tee. It was obvious Tee was a daddy's girl, and she was Gary's heart. The bond grew stronger as she got older. I will always be grateful to Gary for his support, especially where my children were concerned.

Both Von and Tee had Gary's last name, Byndon; even though we were divorced, I kept his last name. Mom took both Tee and Von under her wings as their caretaker while I continued to live reckless. Mom became attached and protective of them. After having Tee, I abstained from using drugs for a couple of months to care for my babies. I eventually returned to injecting heroin sporadically and snorting cocaine a couple times weekly. James and I stayed together a couple of months after the birth of Tee. Everyone who encountered her loved and admired her beauty. I thought Von would be jealous, but he loved his little sister. I would see Von on the bed kissing and hugging her. It was a blessing and was extremely joyful to see them together. I was grateful that God had blessed me with two healthy babies.

I was in the process of leaving James because of so much negative drama between us. Only my drug addiction and money kept me there longer than intended. As we were coming to the end of our relationship, I became acquainted with another young man I had befriended. I remember when I stepped into his trailer, he was sitting on his couch with a huge pit bull. I was afraid of the look of that dog, so he put him in a cage. He asked, "Who are you?" I told him my name. He introduced himself as Frog. He then said, "I would love to have you for my lady." We started dating while I was still in a relationship with James.

One night, James and I were having an intimate moment, and during our romance I called him Frog. He did not say anything at that time, but the next morning James confronted me about it. I walked in the kitchen, where he was standing and drinking alcohol. He began calling me very degrading and profane names. I started crying and apologizing. The confrontation escalated to the point I feared for my life. I was so afraid, trembling, and crying, knowing James had guns in his possession, and I was not sure how this was going to end. He continued to use profane language and calling me demeaning names. He ordered me to get out of his house with a gun in his hand, and I left walking. I left James and started an open relationship with Frog. It was evident that I was magnetic to unhealthy relationships that kept me in a vicious cycle of abuse.

I did not know the relationship with Frog was going to be another terrible and abusive phase of my life's journey. He was also in the business of making fast money. Doing the same thing repeatedly expecting a different outcome defines insanity. I can admit now my choices qualified this definition of insanity! I was addicted to drugs and money and was a magnet for dysfunctional relationships. My codependent relationships with men revealed just how distorted my thinking was and how needy I was. Frog had a reputation of one to fear if you became his enemy. At the beginning of our relationship, I was not giving him any money. I was simply using his drugs and spending his money. I kept myself in this vicious cycle for so long until this street life became a normal way of life. All I was seeking was love, but I searched for it in all the wrong places and among the wrong people. It was obvious my sense of self-worth was declining. I did not love myself and lost touch with my identity, spoken by my mother:' a chosen child.' Those in my circle were just as needy and empty as I was. I am a witness that sin will take you further than you intend to go and will reduce you to the lowest term. Being addicted to drugs and being a lady of the night was nothing I had planned or desired when I was younger.

I remember one night while walking the streets, two of my childhood church friends saw me. They waved at me and stepped out of the car to speak. I was shocked that they would take the time to converse with me. They did not acknowledge what I was doing; they simply saw me as their sister and friend. I tried to mask my shame and pain by jesting and reflecting on childhood memories. I avoided talking about my present state, having a drug problem, and walking the streets. I was miserable and shameful about the way I was living. There was nothing pretty or gratifying about this lifestyle, especially having a drug addiction. Seeing them brought conviction to my heart, but not enough to change my behaviors. The darkness of sin had blinded and hardened my heart, and I was a prisoner of demonic strongholds. There were times I was so delusional, trying to justify and glamorize this lifestyle without acknowledging the risk factors and the pain I suffered. I did not even consider the pain, embarrassment, and disappointments I inflicted upon my family. I had abandoned my children and neglected my parental responsibilities. The devil had camouflaged himself with money, unhealthy relationships, and drugs with the intention of taking my life. I was so deep into my addiction until I felt so hopeless, and I was holding on by a piece of thread.

Things got progressively worse between Frog and me. We would often fight about money and drugs. There were times he forbade me to visit my family. I would go days without talking with my children. Tee and Von continue to live with my family, so I was not worried about their welfare. They especially loved being with Erika, my younger sister. I moved farther away from my parents' location because of my increased criminal activities. I did not want to expose them to any danger because of my illicit behavior and the consequences of my poor decisions. Frog and I continued to commit crimes more frequently to get money to support our addiction. This put a greater demand on me to walking the streets more often and longer. I remember one night, a stranger stopped and asked if I was a lady of the night. I said yes and got into his car. He took me to an area in the woods. When we came to a stop, I looked up, and his fist was in my face. My head bounced back and hit the window of his car. This man put his hand around my throat and pressed on my windpipe until I felt life leaving my body. My bowels broke on the floor of his car while he hit me with the other hand. I pleaded with him, "Please don't kill me! I just had a baby!"

As I was losing consciousness, with the little breath I had left, I whispered, "Lord, save me!" Immediately, I thought about heaven and hell. I thought I was going to die! In a split moment, I recalled the teaching and preaching from my childhood, "Repent and thou shall be saved!" The unidentified stranger saw I was becoming lifeless, and eventually he released my neck. After coming to and catching my breath I thanked him for not killing me and apologized for having a bowel movement in his car. This man was more gratified by inflicting pain and placing me in a near-death state. I attempted to clean myself as much as possible. I know it was God who had commanded this individual to spare my life and demand he drive me back to the location where he had found me. Even though this incident occurred in the early seventies, this experience traumatized me for years because I almost died.

I located Frog and told him what happened. It was obvious someone had attacked me because my face was swollen, and my lip was bleeding. Frog took me home to clean me up and bandaged my wounds. I did not report the incident to the police because the police knew of my reputation on the streets. I did not share it with family members. I knew the high risks and consequences that came with entertaining strangers. I was so grateful God did not allow me to die that night. I do not know where I would have spent eternity. My cry for salvation was prompt out of desperation and fear of dying. I want to believe God's mercy would have saved me, but God's grace and mercy spared my life.

I did not visit my family until my wounds were heal. Guilt and shame overwhelmed my heart each day I stayed away from my children. I would call home to speak to them, trying to ease my guilt. Mom would ask me, "When are you coming here to see these children?" I would give her false hope that it would be the next day or a couple of days, but it would be weeks. My ex-husband, Gary, was still coming around to visit with my family and spend time with Tee. He would give Mom money to help with her and my children's needs. I would also give Mom money and food stamps to help provide for my babies. Providing those food stamps gave me a false sense of fulfilling my parental responsibility as a mother.

In addition to selling drugs, I found myself participating in the crime of robbery to support my addiction. I preferred robbing rather than compromising my body. The devil had hardened my heart to the point of making me fearless and heartless toward victims.

Tee was a year old, and Von was two years old. I recall one night while having my babies at home with me. An incident occurred that awakened me to the reality of just how bad my addiction was. I was preparing to inject heroin into my vein when Von walked into the kitchen and attempted to pick up my drugs. I became so angry and yelled at him because I thought he would spill my heroin on the floor. He left crying, not understanding what had just happened. My thought was that I would deal with him later after I got this heroin in my arm. I neglected attending to my baby, and my priority at the time was getting high. I could no longer deny I had a serious drug problem. I was doing a terrible job managing my life and caring for my children. I chose using drugs over attending to the cry of my baby. I felt remorseful about yelling at him but could not control this monster of addiction. Getting high was my escapism from not only life but also who I had become. After I injected my drug, I went into the bedroom to hug Tee and Von and comfort and love them. I tried to reassure them from any fears. They embraced my hugs and kisses, trying to adjust to my mood changes. I judged myself every day as a terrible mother, but now I know I was an extremely sick mother due to my addiction. I thank God that mom was not far away from where I was living. My parents' home was our sanctuary and safe place. Von and Tee always looked forward to going over to their grandma's house. They especially loved spending time with my younger sister, Erika who was around the same age as Von. She was like a sister to them, and they were close.

One day, I took Von and Tee to their grandma's house so Frog and I could go out to get money through illicit activities. When we returned home, our apartment was on fire and burned down to the ground. The fire consumed everything I possessed. Frog and I got a hotel room for a couple of weeks, and my children remained with Mom. The investigation concluded the fire was arson. Someone had set our apartment on fire. I suspected Frog and I had made enemies along the way related to our illicit activities. Frog and I had to find another residence. I finally found another apartment closer to my parents' house. Moving closer to my parents made it convenient for childcare when I needed it. I allowed my children to live with Mom for a couple of weeks until we were into our new apartment. Tee and Von loved the idea of being closer to their grandparents. Once settled, we continued the same illegal activities at our new location.

On a Friday night a couple of months into living at our new location, Frog and I decided to go out to party. I took my babies to spend the night with my parents. As I was walking the streets, an unfamiliar stranger asked me for entertainment. Rather than entertaining the young man, Frog and I decided to rob him. I did not know that this crime was about to cost me my freedom and could result in me going to prison. We robbed people at other times, and we thought this was going to be as other times, a clean getaway.

CHAPTER 6

Arrested with My Baby in My Arms

THE FOLLOWING WEEK, I WAS WALKING FROM THE NEIGHBORHOOD STORE with Tee in my arms and Von walking beside me when an undercover detective drove up behind me. He stopped, got out of the police car, and asked me, "Are you Christine Byndon?" I responded, "yes sir." The detective said, "Mrs. Byndon, you have been identified as a suspect in an armed robbery crime." The detective allowed me to call someone to get my children. I tried to comfort my children and assure them I would be right back. They were too young to comprehend what was going on, so they willingly went with a neighbor to my parents' house a couple blocks away. The detective handcuffed me in the presence of my children and put me in the back of his police car. My first arrest was for solicitation, which was a misdemeanor, but this was a felony. They locked me in jail on a felony charge. The detective was kind and respectful toward me. He started asking me questions about Frog and told me that they had arrested him for the same felony charge.

Now, I was facing prison time for an armed robbery charge! In the process of the arrest, I found out Frog had other outstanding warrants. When it came time for my first court appearance, the court appointed me a state appointed attorney because I could not afford an attorney. The judge placed me on a ten-thousand-dollars bond, and the bailer took me back to my jail cell. During my first meeting with my attorney, he informed me of a plea bargaining offer the state prosecutor was willing to accept. They offer to reduce my charge from felony robbery to common-law robbery. I said yes and accepted the plea bargaining because I knew I did not have a chance with the state prosecutor. I was sure a jury would not favor me because of my reputation. I remained in jail for a couple of weeks. While I was in jail mom would bring Tee and Von into the parking lot of the jailhouse so I could see them from the window. I would take a white towel and wave it from the jailhouse window to let Mom know I could see them. Mom would point toward the jail window so Von and Tee would look up and see me waving a white towel, and they waved back at me. It broke my heart to not be able to hug my babies. My mom never forsook me, but she never condoned or enabled my addiction and the consequences of my poor decisions. Even when Dad wanted to use their house as collateral to get me out on the ten-thousand-dollars bond, Mom refused to get me out because she knew it was time for me to face consequences. She would visit me in jail when she could.

I remember the day I stood in front of the judge for his ruling. Mom and Dad sat behind me in the courtroom for support. When the judge read my sentence and the amount of time I would spend in prison, I heard my mother crying and saw dad holding her firmly in his arms. The judge said, "Christine Byndon, you are sentenced to four to six years confinement in the North Carolina Women's Correctional Center for common-law robbery."

Mom was crying and calling my name saying, "No! Chris!" It felt like my heart fell to the floor after hearing the agony of my mother's cry. I caused my mom so much pain, but this moment was almost unbearable for both of us. Dad held Mom tightly while embracing her in his arms. Tears poured from my eyes hearing the agony of my mother's cry and thinking of the separation from my children for that amount of time. Remorse filled my heart but there was nothing I could have verbalize to resolve this. The bailiff took me back upstairs to my jail cell. That night I must have cried myself to sleep because that morning my pillow was soaking wet from my tears. They scheduled me for transport to the correctional center within a couple of days. While waiting for transportation to the prison facility, a Social Worker from Child Protective Services visited my parent's house. They informed mom that my parental rights were going to be taking away because of my confinement in prison, and they were investigating appropriate caretakers for my children. I heard that mom said to that Social Worker, "Nobody is going to take my grandchildren. If I must eat beans every night, my grandchildren will eat beans also!" My grandchildren will stay here with me!" The social worker had me sign over my parental rights to my parents.

After processing my thoughts and feelings, without any doubt it was in the plan of God for me to go to prison for safekeeping because of all the near-death encounters, and God was preparing me for His divine purpose. The reality set in as they transported me from the county jail to prison for four to six years. "I am a criminal, and my freedom is gone!" When I arrived at the prison facility the women were standing in the yard looking at us as we got out of the van. Once I entered the prison gate, I heard women calling my name: "Christine!" They were women I knew from walking the streets. I was not nervous, just regretful that I had lost my freedom. The lifestyle I had engaged in prepared me to deal with the prison mentality, and my reputation preceded me. I went in with a hardcore mentality because I was determined nobody was going to violate or bully me.

After four weeks, my mom came to visit with me, and she brought my baby girl, Tee. I cannot remember who else came with her. My mom would go to any length to keep my children in my life and remain supportive. When she came to visit me, I was proud to announce that my mom was a preacher, and I made it known I came from good stock. My parents would visit regularly, and they made sure I had money for the canteen to buy snacks. Mom obtained favor with the superintendent, who allowed her and a prayer team to come inside the prison to do Bible study and sing songs with the other inmates. The inmates would come to hear mom teach the Word of God. Ladies accepted Christ as their personal Savior through her teaching of the Word of God. What intended to be an unpleasant situation for me had resulted as a soul saving encounter for other inmates behind the walls of prison. Glory to God!

Both Slim and Frog wrote to me from different prison camps. Wherever I went, my demons followed me. There were drugs available on the grounds, so my addiction was still active. I received write ups for infractions during my imprisonment. I became one of the negative influential leaders in prison and I had the respect on the grounds from other inmates. There was a riot within the prison among the inmates, and I partook. There was a confrontation between correctional officers and the inmates, resulting in property damage and injuries to both parties. They charged and punished me for my participation in the riot. I was place in isolation for seven days. I lost visitation privileges for a couple weekends.

When it was time for my parole review and consideration. The parole board denied it because of my participation in the riot. Mom was disappointed to hear of my involvement in the protest and the denial of my parole. After a week, I was able to return to the grounds but had another week before I could have visitors. I returned to my duties working in the kitchen. As time progressed, I started missing my children and grew tired of confinement. I worked hard to stay out of trouble and separated myself from the troublemakers. The weekend came when I could have visitors, and my mom was at the gate with my children and sisters. I heard inmates yelling across the yard, "Christine, your mother is here to see you!" Those ladies were so excited to see my mom just as I was because she blessed their lives when she came to minister God's Word and pray with them.

After spending two years in prison, my parole came up again for the second time. I was a little nervous of rejection again for parole because I had a couple more of writeups for infractions. Overall, I had made improvements in my attitude, attended Narcotics Anonymous (NA) support meetings, and earned gain-time working in the kitchen. I had an acceptable home plan which was to reside with my parents. When I met with the parole board, it was a different group of officials, and they were impressed with the report of my progress and my home plan. They approved and recommended my parole. My release date was within a couple of weeks.

When released from prison, I was not release from the demonic strongholds that enslaved me throughout my addiction and unhealthy relationships. I still had that sinful nature even though I was saying all the right things. I simply articulated an acceptable plan to get out of prison. My desires were to make up for lost time with my children and family. Even if I wanted to change the way I was living, I lacked the will to do so. Frog remained in prison serving twelve to fifteen years. This was my opportunity to break free from him and take control of my life to pursue a productive lifestyle. Throughout my confinement, Frog and I were still conversing through mail. He was happy my parole came through because he expected me to visit and support him. I could not deny him because I felt a sense of commitment to him even though it was an abusive relationship.

Finally, the day came for my released from prison. They gave me the conditions of my parole requirements, a contact name, and a date to report to the parole office. As a condition of my parole, I had to follow up with a referral to a community resource for vocational rehabilitation. As I prepared to leave out, I heard the conversation of a couple of the ladies saying, "She'll be back!" When I walked out of those gates, I was not looking back to say bye to anyone. My parents and my babies were waiting for me outside the gates. It was so good to be able to hug my babies and return home with my parents. Being able to walk in the free world once again was like the excitement and extraordinary joy children experience on a celebratory day. Being with my children and my family was the greatest gift I could receive on the day of my release.

For the first couple of months, I stayed home spending quality time with my children and my family. I reported to the parole office as mandated to review my release plan and give a status report. My family time spent with my babies and siblings was priceless. It was a celebratory moment with laughter and feelings of gratitude to have another chance to be together as we embraced one another. That bonding time was necessary to make amends and bring healing. I had to regain their trust after years of neglect and abandonment.

I received a letter from Frog expressing his love for me and asking me to visit him. Frog also informed me that he had received a transfer to a prison camp closer to my location. I did not own transportation, so I had to arrange for transportation to visit him. I knew Mom forbidden me from visiting Frog and it would be in violation of my parole conditions. I loved him and felt like I owed him my support. When I visited with him, we were both glad to see each other and talked about potential plans after his release. Frog kept telling me, "I am not staying here twelve to fifteen years!" I knew he would be in prison for a while unless God gave him a miracle, or he was planning an escape. He did not share any plans to do so. I gave Frog a couple of dollars and promised him I would return. I knew I was putting my freedom at risk, but I convinced myself I simply had to take precaution when visiting him.

CHAPTER 7

On the Run

THREE MONTHS PASSED SINCE MY RELEASE, AND I HAD NOT USED ANY drugs. My sobriety was not because of the lack of cravings, because I certainly had them. It was because I was not sure when a parole officer was going to show up. One of my parole conditions mandated me to submit urine testing. Except for visiting Frog, I tried to walk a tightrope and comply with parole requirements to avoid returning to prison for three more years. The more I visited with Frog, the more it became obvious he had no plan to serve all his time, and he might be planning an escape from prison. He did not share his plan with me; we simply discussed plans when we reunite after his release.

One day, Frog called me and informed me that he had escaped from prison. I was in shock, and I would be a suspect concerning his escape. I was now in violation of my parole and at risk of going back to prison. I was determined I was not returning to prison, so I left town without informing anyone. I relocated to New York. I was still communicating with Frog and gave him the telephone number where I was residing. Not long after Frog called and informed me that he was in New York. I made plans to meet him at a location, and we ended up taking the train to Newark, New Jersey. We got a room in a hotel for a couple of nights. Our funds were low, so I was back in the streets participating in illegal activities to get money. I was so scared because I was in a strange land with no familiar connections. I was not familiar with the city at all, so I felt very vulnerable. Frog had to keep a low profile because he was a fugitive. Conflicts increased between Frog and me, living from day to day and not knowing where we were going to sleep each night. Getting money was entirely on me, and Frog sought out drugs so we could get high.

There were two memorable events that occurred while I was in Newark. One night a stranger asked me for entertainment. I got in his car not knowing where he was taking me or how to get back to my location. He took me to an unfamiliar location, and there was another man at the house waiting for him. They preceded to rape me, and I heard them planning to keep me there. When they turned their heads, I got hold of my clothes and barely dressed, I ran out of the house. They came running after me. I noticed strangers walking down the sidewalk in the direction I was running, and I cried to them, "Please help me! They're trying to hurt me!" The strangers confronted them in my defense, and they started fighting. There was a car passing, and I asked this stranger who was driving alone, "Please help me!" He allowed me to jump into his car and drove off. I told him that I needed to go back to town. He tried to flirt with me after discovering I was unfamiliar with the area. God touched his heart to carry me directly in town. He dropped me off, and I saw Frog walking around looking for me. I knew it was my mother's prayers that had intervened for me again, along with God's grace and mercy.

We remained in Newark for about a week. I got a charge for solicitation within that week. I resisted the arrest and used profane language at the police. When they locked me up, they stripped me from all I had on which included my clothes, my wig, and my makeup. I was so ashamed and embarrassed, feeling completely naked. When I stood before the judge, he asked me, "Do you live here?"

I responded, "No Sir."

"Where did you come from?" he asked.

I said, "Sir, I came from New York."

He said to me, "I'm not going to lock you up, but I am going to give you sundown to get out of my town!" I left the courtroom relieved and grateful for not getting any jail time. Frog was waiting for me outside the courthouse.

We packed our bags and traveled to Augusta, Georgia. We had no family members or connections there, so it was another strange land for me. We could not return home because we both had warrants out for our arrests. I would call my parents every now and then, but I would not tell them where I was located. Every call home was a collect call from a pay phone. I knew if the police would question Mom about my whereabouts, she was not going to lie to protect me, so I kept my location from her. I would ask her to let me speak to my babies. While speaking to Von, he would ask me, "When are you coming home, Mom?" Their little voices would melt my heart, and I would feel bad about abandoning them again.

Frog and I would walk the streets looking for means to get money and drugs. We had enough money to get a motel room for about three days, but there were a couple of days when we were homeless and hungry. I walked the streets as much as I could until I became physically sick. Pain plagued my body to the point I could barely walk. To my surprise, I was pregnant and was experiencing morning sickness. I told Frog that I thought I was pregnant. He was excited because he had never had a child. Even though I told him I was pregnant, he still expected me to get money by any means necessary. Our drug addiction took priority over my body pains and medical disposition.

One night, Frog asked me to go out to engage in illicit activities to get money for drug use. I said, "No! I do not feel good!" Despite my pain, I went out because we needed money. I walked up and down the streets with tears flowing down my face and pain penetrating throughout my body. I stayed out about an hour and returned to the hotel without money in my hand. After I returned to the room, Frog left. He eventually returned with money and drugs. We had just enough money for one more night in the motel. My body pains became so unbearable. The next morning, I made a collect call to my mother, and she accepted the call as always. I told her how sick I was and stated I had no money. Mom asked me, "Where are you?" I told her of my location. We were about to be homeless within two days by checkout time, and I was not looking forward to that or walking the streets. Every time I called home, Mom would tell me, "I love you." She then asked, "Where do you want me to send the money?" I gave her the address to the motel where we were staying. I could barely walk back to the room because of the pain; I was so sick. I told Frog I had called my mom to send me money for medication and food. He did not argue with me because he could see I was sick and getting worse. The only two things that could give me any relief was lying down in a certain position on my sides and drugs. I would inject heroin to help relieve my pain. I was not considering my pregnancy at the time; I simply wanted relief from my misery.

CHAPTER 8

A Divine Intervention

THE NEXT MORNING, I HEARD A KNOCK ON OUR MOTEL DOOR. IT WAS MY ex-husband, my sister Gwen, and my daughter. Instead of sending the money, mom had sent Gary to bring me home. Even though Gary and I were divorced, he continued to stay connected with my family, especially Tee, our daughter. I stepped outside the motel room to speak to them. Frog remained in the room. I could barely walk without bending over. I returned inside the room and told Frog that I was going home. He did not want me to leave, but he knew he could not help me. I was in severe pain and needed medical attention. God softened Frog's heart to permit me to leave. As I prepared to leave Frog, it was a sad departure for us. I was so ashamed for my daughter and my ex-husband to see me like this, but I was grateful they had come to get me. I knew if I could just get back in the presence of my mom's loving arms, everything would be all right.

There was little conversation as we traveled back to my parent's house. Tee was in the back seat with me. She reached out to me and kissed me, and I embraced her with all the strength my weak body could release. I was so glad to see my pretty little baby. They stopped to pick up food as I continued to rest in the back seat. Gary never judged me but was very caring and kind as we traveled back home. That Friday evening when we got to my parents' house, I noticed Mom opening the door and coming out with a big smile on her face, and with her arms wide open. "Come on in, Chris," she said with a trembling voice, and tears filled her eyes. She hugged and kissed me. My babies ran up to me to hug me. As soon as I stepped into my mom's anointed atmosphere, my pain began to subside, and my body gained strength. I felt a sense of security, peace, and comfort at being back home. Everyone there was glad to see me and loved me. I knew I looked bad because of the lack of sleep, sick body, and weight loss due to my addiction. I had brought a bag of heroin and paraphernalia with me so I would not go into withdrawals. By this time, I had not had any drugs for twenty-four hours. Mom began to pray for me, rebuking every demonic attack that was coming against my body and mind. She started speaking in tongues in her heavenly language and pleading the blood of Jesus Christ over my life. God immediately and miraculously healed me, and the sickness and every pain left my body. Strength overcame me, and I felt renewed. Tears ran down my face not only because the pain was gone from my body, but also because I felt overwhelmed with gratitude for being back home with my family. Everything I suffered and every near-death experience I escaped was by the grace and mercies of God.

My mom welcomed me home and showed me unconditional love. She went into the kitchen to get me something to eat, and we talked as if I had never left home. Mom was always known as a prayer warrior, and she was the devil's worst nightmare. When she prayed, I am sure her prayers shook the gates of hell. God always manifested His power on her behalf when she prayed. After I finished eating, Mom told me to wash up, lie down, and rest. I could not remember the last time I was able to rest in perfect peace. My dad was home when I arrived, and he did not say much, but I knew he was glad to have me home by the big smile on his face. He said, "Hey, stranger!" I knew Mom went on long days of fasting and praying for my safe return home, and I thanked her. I slept throughout the night without any disturbances.

I woke up by the sound of laughter, my children running down the hallway and the smell of bacon. Mom was in the kitchen cooking breakfast. It was a celebratory moment of my return home. It brought to memory the story in the Bible recorded in Luke 15:11–32 (KJV) about the prodigal son. My parents' love reflected the love of the father in this parable. After eating breakfast with my family, I spent the remainder of the day laughing and playing with my children. I did not immediately tell mom of my pregnancy. I had not received any prenatal care and was injecting heroin every day before coming home, and I was concerned about the health of my unborn baby. The second day of my return home continued to be celebratory with my family with laughter, eating, and playing with my children. I was experiencing physical discomfort, but it was bearable. That Saturday evening, Mom was on the phone talking with Vertell, one of my childhood friends. I heard Mom rejoicing as she shared about me being home. When she finished speaking with Vertell, she approached me about attending church with her on Sunday evening. I wanted to say no because I was still struggling with guilt and shame.

Vertell called back to speak with me personally. During our phone conversation, she said, "Hi, how are you doing? I hope you will come tomorrow; my husband will be preaching." Her voice was so pleasant and so embracing. I felt less resistant and was more willing to accept her invitation. Before getting off the phone with her, I promised her I would come to the service. I always looked up to Vertell as a friend and a big sister. I respected her for upholding Christian standards, and she was the epitome of a lady with grace and beauty.

The people within our church community knew about my drug problem, my confinement in prison, and me being a lady of the night. Despite my shame, I felt obligated to both mom and Vertell. This was the least I could do for all the sacrifices Mom had made for me. I was appreciative of the love, patience, and forgiveness she had shown me through the years. It was my mom who was the caretaker of my children every time I abandoned them. I returned home only because of the affliction that totally disabled me physically. This crisis and affliction were the vehicle orchestrated by God as a divine intervention to bring me back home for salvation.

During my discussion with Mom about going to church, I told her if I ever accepted Christ in my life again, I would not be a hypocrite or backslider. I reckoned I wanted her to know that her prayers were working on me. I also told her there might be a warrant for my arrest for parole violation. She encouraged me to come to church and said, "God will work it out." I had not used the drugs that I had brought back with me. Later that day, I had Dad buy me a carton of Kool cigarettes. My intention was to use that bag of drugs when I got back from church. I finally told Mom I was pregnant before going to church. Mom gave me one of her dresses to wear to church because wearing pants were not acceptable in our family church.

It was Sunday morning, and everyone was preparing for church. I stayed home with one of my siblings and my babies. When they returned from morning service, we ate dinner. As time drew closer for evening service, I was anxious about going, but I was determined to not go back on my promise made to Mom and my friend Vertell. When I walked into church, it felt like everyone's eyes were on me. I took a seat in the back of the church, with my children seated beside me. Reverend John Godbolt preached a powerful word about the love of God, and it ministered to my spirit. I could feel the presence of God come upon me. I felt a breaking in my spirit, but I also could feel a spiritual warring going on within me. The demonic strongholds were tightening their grip on me. I could feel the spirit of the Lord rising and working inside my heart. At the end of the message, the preacher made an altar call. I had already decided I was not going to the altar. My mindset was, "I have too many issues that need to be resolved before I make a commitment to God." I sat there trying hard to resist the pulling of the Holy Spirit. Reverend Godbolt said to the church, "All I am led to do is lay my hands upon you."

The devil was in my ear, discouraging me from going to the altar. All I could hear was the devil saying, "Don't go! You are not ready! You can't do it now!" The devil was reminding me of my struggles and my relationship with Frog.

I felt the Spirit of the Lord lifting me up from my seat, and before I realized what was happening, I found myself walking down the aisle toward the altar. I said to myself, "I will just let him lay hands upon me," asking God to fix my problems, especially the risk of going back to prison. Understand that I simply wanted God to get me out of trouble, but I was not willing to come out of my sins. I made it through the prayer line without making a commitment to God. I convinced myself I was not ready to accept Christ, because I relied on my own ability to fix my life. As I was walking toward the altar, it felt like I was dragging chains on my ankles. I could feel the weight of demonic forces holding me hostage. I returned to my seat, but the tears were still falling down my face.

As soon as I sat down, Reverend Godbolt looked toward me and called my name, asking me, "Sister Chris, can I pray for you again?" God allowed this preacher to shine the spotlight on me. I said yes and walked to the front of the church. He started ministering to my spirit and asked me, "Would you like to give God your life tonight?"

I quickly said, "No! I am not ready." The spiritual battle I was experiencing intensified, and there was a warring between my flesh against the spirit. The devil was in my ear, saying no. But I felt a breaking within, and my heart was melting.

I felt a fresh wind blowing over me, and I heard the Spirit of God speak in my ears, "Christine, if not tonight, there will be no other night!" As the tears flowed down my face, the power of the Holy Spirit parted my lips, and I began to ask God to save me. Hallelujah! Glory to God!

The preacher asked me again, "Do you want to accept Christ in your life as your personal Savior?"

I said, "Yes!" loudly and tearfully. I cried out of my soul to God, "Save me," and I thanked Him for my deliverance. Hallelujah! Glory to God! God saved me that night in 1978.

It seemed like everyone in the church was shouting and praising God with me and for me. I had not felt so light and liberated in my spirit and mind for a long time. I was so full of joy that I praised God all the way home. When I got to my parent's house, I flushed the bag of heroin and broke up all the cigarettes and flushed them too. I got my paraphernalia and threw it in the woods. I said aloud, "Goodbye to it all!" I did not need detoxification because God had given me a transformation. God totally transformed me by the power of God. Praise God!

Later that night after church, when I arrived at home, I received a phone call from Frog. Frog said to me, "I'm back in town. Come over." He wanted me to meet him, but I refused.

I told him that I had accepted Christ in my life. "I got saved tonight!" I told him I was ending our relationship and could not see him anymore.

He pleaded and begged me to come over. He said to me, "Christine, I am happy for you. I will go to church with you." I told him no firmly and hung up the phone. It was truly over because I was serious about maintaining my commitment to God. Glory to God! I know it was God who had snatched the desire to be with him out of my heart, and He took residence on the throne of my heart. What a great victory! I felt overwhelmed with gratitude for my conversion that I did not want to sleep that night. I was in bed looking toward heaven, and tears flowed down my face with gratitude. That same night, God gave me a song that comforted me about issues concerning my parole violation. The name of the song that God gave me was "If the Lord Can't Fix It, Nobody Can." God was ministering to my heart through that song, reassuring me that everything was going to be all right. I got up the next morning singing this song. Mom and I started praising God together right there in the kitchen.

Vertell and Reverend John Godbolt became my spiritual mentors. They took interest in my spiritual growth and invested their time to keep me encouraged. I would spend time at their house and attend church services with them when I could. My family was so happy for me because they did not have to worry about my well-being because I was no longer on the streets. The power of my mom's prayers came to fruition, and I was finally home and born again by the power of God. Every chance I had; I told my mom thanks for not giving up on me. The devil had me in his dungeon, but the blood of Jesus penetrated through the fortress of demonic territory and delivered me. Hallelujah! I was determined I would be faithful to God and be a witness and a warrior against the kingdom of the devil.

Every time the church doors were open, I was in attendance. My friend Vertell went into her personal closet and gave me nice outfits to wear to church. I discarded everything that reminds me of my past, even my clothing. My aim was to be a holy woman of God and to look like a lady, not a woman of the night. Immediately I started crucifying flesh by going on personal fasts, staying in prayer, and detaching myself from unsaved friends and family members with whom I use to run the streets with.

I am a living testimony of why one should never judge anyone before time. I finally received medical care to check on the status of my pregnancy and received a good report. I also praised God for the report of being negative for sexually transmitted diseases despite my promiscuous behaviors. I want to encourage and inspire the chosen sons and daughters, the Joshua's generation who are presently taking this same journey: Your destiny is calling for you to come back home! It might look like you are at a point of no return, but prayer can reach wherever you are. My mom's prayer was as a spiritual hook, my lifeline that snatched me out of the snares of the devil, death, and hell. Praise God! I say to those who have gone astray, "Come back home, prodigal child!" You are one of those chosen ones assigned for greatness and for a kingdom purpose.

CHAPTER 9

My Commitment Tried in the Fire

I STAYED WITH MY PARENTS UNTIL I GAVE BIRTH TO YOLANDA. AGAIN, I was able to apply for welfare assistance. This allowed me to have a monthly check, food stamps, and Medicaid for medical care. Mom and I had a talk about restoring my parental rights for Tee and Von. Mom observed and discerned that I was sincere about serving God, as evidenced by my pursuit for Him and my lifestyle change. She felt comfortable returning the custody of my children to me.

My mother assists me with applying for housing under the Department of Housing and Urban Development (HUD) for low-income recipients not too far from her. They approved my application for an apartment that same day, but I had to wait until an apartment was available to move into. A couple of weeks later, we went to Child Protective Services requesting consideration to restore custody of my children back to me. After the review of my case, they reinstated my parental rights. The day I went to get my babies, Tee started crying, and I heard her saying to my mom, "I don't want to go with her!"

Mom said, "Tee, that's your mother. You and Von go with her. It's okay!" My heart dropped within with sadness, but I could not blame her because my mom and family were there in my absence providing love and security for both my children. Once I got my children to our new home, I attempted to shower them with love and affection. I would buy them extra things trying to compensate for the past and establish a bond of trust. I reckon one would say I tried to buy their love to make amends. I simply wanted them to know that I was remorseful for abandoning them and that

I loved them. It was my desire to make them feel secure in being with me. It was not a smooth transition for my children to leave their grandma, but they knew she was close by. Once God restored our relationship, I spent quality time with them to form a stronger bond. After getting a little more stable in my own apartment, I enrolled in a general educational development (GED) program at a local community college. My dream was to go to college to become a substance abuse counselor. When I did complete the GED program, I gave my high school diploma to my mom as an act of making amends. My parents were so proud of me, especially my mom. I still had a felony on my record, and I lost citizenship rights, which made it hard to gain job opportunities and so much more. However, they directed me to seek community services through the Vocational Rehabilitation Services (VRS), which helped with finding employment and educational opportunities for felony offenders. Thank God I qualified for their services. I was able to gain assistance from their resources. This program offered me the tools and resources that empowered me in becoming a productive citizen and enhanced my personal growth. I remember taking an academic placement test that evaluated college readiness. I failed the test and the instructor recommend me to seek more tutoring and preparation in certain subject matters. This news was discouraging but I still maintained my faith and remained surrounded by the prayer warriors, especially my mom. After twelve weeks of tutoring and completing additional educational courses through the Vocational Rehabilitation Services, I resubmitted my application for admission and Fayetteville State University accepted my admission. This was the highlight of my life and a terrific opportunity for me to pursue a college degree. God continued to open doors for me and crown me with favor before men. I was able to work in the psychology department under work study with the psychology professors. You know that was God's favor!

My transportation to school every day was the city bus for a year. When I got my school refund from my school grant, I was able to buy my first car. I was so grateful about the open doors and the favors God had shown toward me. I enrolled Von and Tee into kindergarten, and I enrolled Yolanda in the daycare on the college campus. That made it convenient for me while in school.

I continued to be faithful in my church attendances to strengthen my faith as I gained stability as a Christ follower. Whatever my mother, my pastor, and those seasoned church mothers told me to do, I did it without questioning. I knew my triggers and strongholds that kept me in bondage, and I was determined not to be yoke up again! I was not going to tempt God or put myself in a compromising position. Those church mothers were covering and protecting us from the demonic warfare forces. They had the anointing to drive back the spirit of darkness and every demonic attack that came against us. Yes, they knew how to plead the blood against demons. All they had to say was, "Loose here with authority," and the yokes of the devil were loose. It was necessary for me to remain under that kind of power and covering to maintain my deliverance from demonic strongholds. After I received the Holy Ghost, God gave me that same power. The young adults within our church had such a passion and a strong pursuit for God, which enabled me to be steadfast in my deliverance. I spent quality time at house prayer meetings, and sometimes we had all-night prayer meetings. I would pray consistently in my apartment early in the mornings, and I attended noonday and sometimes all-night prayer. I had my prayer closet in Tee's bedroom because that was the largest closet in my apartment. According to St. Matthew 5:6 (KJV), "Blessed are they which do hunger and thirst after righteousness: for they shall be filled." Praise God!

Things were going great for me in every area of my life until God permitted my faith to go through a fiery trial. I experienced the greatest test of my life after going strong in church for three years. I was getting closer to my last semester in college before graduation. By this time, Yolanda was three years old. My three children, Von, Tee, and Yolanda, and I had attended church on a Palm Sunday. The most challenging, painful, and devastating moment I ever experienced happened on this celebratory sacred day. My three-year-old baby girl, Yolanda died right in front of the church after the closing of morning service.

The week just before her death, we had a revival at my home church. The revivalist, the late Apostle Sessions, was a powerful and anointed man of God. On the last night of the revival, he preached so hard under the anointing until his clothes were soaking wet. The power of God was heavy upon him. His sermon was "Ain't No Telling!" The anointing and the power of God moved so greatly; the Holy Spirit had slayed us to the floor and the power of the Holy Ghost poured upon the young and old.

The fire of the Holy Spirit sat upon me, and I was having an out-of-body experience. I got so drunk in the spirit that my spiritual parents drove me home and help me upstairs to my apartment. I believed at that time God was preparing my spirit for my daughter's death, which happened the following week.

I remember the events that led up to Yolanda's death that Sunday morning like it was yesterday. Everyone nearby in my community knew I was a Christian and a single parent. They also knew I was a praying lady because my neighbors would tell me they heard me praying and crying out early in the mornings and late at nights. I stayed in my "prayer closet." When Tee was sleeping, I would make my altar in the living room. I can remember early one morning around 3:00 a.m., I was up weeping and praying so hard (travailing, as a woman in labor) until my cry woke up Yolanda. She came into the living room crying and fell in my lap. I held her in my arms and rubbed her little head on my shoulder to comfort her, but I continued to intensively pray. I had a real passion for God and so much gratitude during this time because of my deliverance from drugs, and I was grateful for having my children and having a second chance to live free from my demons.

I always stayed on guard and was vigilant for any temptation or attacks of the devil attempting to overtake me. I armed myself with prayer and the Word of God and determined that nothing would break my fellowship with God! I was so protective of my salvation that I would not even allow Yolanda's biological father to visit with her until she was around two years old, which was his only time. He was still a fugitive. I knew what I had to do to protect my salvation and my children. I lived in proximity to my pastor, the late Bishop Townsend, and Mother Townsend; they were my spiritual parents and they kept me covered in the spirit. Every chance I got during testimony services, I would jump up to praise God for my deliverance and testify how God had delivered me from a miserable life of sin.

I would have never imagined losing my three-year-old baby in a tragic accident would be in the plan of God, especially after accepting Him as my Savior. I knew my testimony and commitment to God would cost me, but not at the price of losing my daughter. I had Yolanda dressed so pretty in her green dress and white shoes. That Sunday morning, I felt so heavy but was not sure why. Even during the praise service, I struggled with a heavy spirit. God was dealing with my spirit to warn me of trouble. That Sunday morning, everyone was praising God, singing, shouting, and dancing in the spirit. Yolanda was praising God in the dance along with the saints. Even though Yolanda was three years old, her spirit had direct connection to the Spirit of God that day. I could see the Spirit of God all over her face as she was raising her hands and dancing in the spirit. She was so energetic, dancing and clapping her hands. She jumped up and down in the aisle and praised God so radically. I told her, "Yolanda, sit down!"

Someone said, "Leave her alone and let her praise God." So, I just let her dance and praise God. I had never witnessed Yolanda praise God so intensely in church. As you may remember, I attended one of those hand clapping, foot-stomping, and tongue-talking churches.

As the late Bishop Townsend was about to end his sermon, the prophetic anointing came upon him. He said, "The Lord is leading me to pray. I sense something is about to happen!" He then requested, "Saints, I want everyone to come around the altar for prayer. I just want to lay hands upon you!" Our pastor had us get in a line so he could lay hands upon everyone. Before I could lift my head, Yolanda had already run to the altar. Pastor was unable to lay hands upon her because she ran to the altar and back to her seat so fast. Our pastor started praying for all the families, binding up demonic attacks, and asking God for divine protection. The pastor gave the benediction after praying. The women's department of the church had a brief meeting and I attend. My children had walked out of the church with family members.

When the meeting was over, I approached the entrance of the doorway to walk out of the church. I heard a loud impact that sounded like a collision, I heard people yelling and crying, and I saw people running down the street yelling. I heard my daughter Tee crying and yelling, "You hit my sister!" She was calling Yolanda's name. Von was standing on the side of the road in front of the church, crying hysterically and in total shock, saying nothing. People were running behind a car that was still moving down the street. I was hysterical and devastated. I started running with the flow of the crowd, asking, "What happened?"

My question was, "How did this happen?" Yolanda had broken away from her brother's hand attempting to get to my sister Gwen on the other side of the street, and she had run in front of the moving car. My baby's body was stuck under that car and dragged for about ninety feet. Once the car released her body from under the car, it was evident that Yolanda had suffered extensive damage to her head and burned over eighty percent of her body.

As people tried to hold me back, I saw my mom running past me and dropping to her knees beside Yolanda's dying body. She lifted Yolanda's lifeless body up, crying and calling her name repeatedly. "Yolanda! Yolanda! Yolanda!" I approached her body, and one of the church mothers, the late Mother James tried to comfort me, I am sure with good intentions, and said to me, "She's going to be alright." We did not know Yolanda was dying right then.

I could barely look at my dying daughter because of her burned body, and her two-and-a-half-foot body had stretched one and half feet longer from being drag under that car. Everyone around me was crying out loudly and screaming. Yolanda was gasping for breath, barely breathing. I could not move and just gazed at Mom tearfully calling her name. I heard one of the ministers of the church say to someone in the crowd, as Mom attempted to pick Yolanda's lifeless body up, "Stop her, don't let her pick her up!" I was in shock and hysterical.

The emergency medical services (EMS) came and put Yolanda inside the ambulance, trying to revive her. I attempted to jump inside the ambulance, but I heard the EMS person say, "Somebody get her from getting in, she cannot ride with us!" Someone within the crowd embraced me and put me in their car. Police cars were coming from everywhere to investigate the scene of the accident.

When I arrived at the hospital, I remember the nurse escorting me into a room while the doctors tried to save Yolanda's life. My mom and others from the church were in the waiting room away from me. While in that isolated room alone, I prayed and asked God, "Is my baby going to be alright?"

Immediately I felt a calmness settling within my spirit, and I sensed in the spirit the peace of God. I heard a whisper in my spirit that softly said, "Yolanda is with me." Even before the doctor and the nurse came into the room where I was waiting, God had sent a fresh wind into that room, and it came over me. God prepared me for the doctor's report. I was the only one in the room when a doctor and a nurse came in to tell me that they could not save Yolanda. I walked out in tears and fell into the arms of my mother. There were others there with Mom to console both of us. When I left the hospital, I returned home to be with Von and Tee and to tell them that Yolanda had transitioned to be with the Lord. Our church family had gathered inside and outside my apartment to comfort my children and waiting to embrace me. When I got in the house I fell on the couch in the front room, and Von fell on the floor beside me, rubbing my head and singing a spiritual song. Every time someone would close the front door, it startled me, and my heart jumped each time. It was if I was hearing the impact from the car accident. I cried myself to sleep. Von remained sitting on the floor where I was lying, rubbing my head, and holding my hand. There was Christian music playing, and I heard Von trying to sing along with the music. I could not imagine how deeply this had affected Tee and Von, who had witnessed the car accident. Tee was nine and Von was ten.

The devil's plan was to break my spirit and break my fellowship with God. I am sure there were people wondering whether this incident would drive me back to drugs and bondage of sin. Going back was not an option! I thank God for the foundational teaching that anchored me firmly to my faith and sealed my commitment to God through this fiery trial.

The thief cometh not, but for to steal, and to kill, and to destroy: I
am come that they might have life, and that
they might have it more abundantly.
(John 10:10 KJV)

I had moments of grief, but I did not give myself permission to deal with my pain openly because I was still in disbelief. I tried extremely hard to be spiritual throughout this experience. I was denying the humanity side of my person to embrace my pain. I was taught it was not acceptable to ask God why, so I tried to be spiritual before man, but privately I questioned God, "Why did this happen to me? Why did God allow this to happen to my baby during the most sacred time of serving Him?" So many emotions and so many questions of whys. I counted myself blessed to have my praying mother and my church family right by my side. They all spoke life and strength into me and kept me lifted with encouraging words. When the enemy came to overtake my mind, God's grace sustained me.

I can remember one day while alone at home, the devil brought suicidal thoughts to my mind and a plan to end my life. Behind my apartment were railroad tracks. The devil tried to persuade me to go stand on the tracks and allow the train to run over me. I did not entertain those thoughts because I had to live for my other two children. Everyone who was aware of my testimony witnessed my perseverance, and they respected and admired my transformation. This tragedy devastated my entire family. My sister Evelyn was terribly upset about losing her niece, and my sister, Gwen felt responsible because Yolanda was attempting to come to her when the accident occurred. The grace and mercies of God sustained me through this troublesome time. I felt like Von blamed himself as well for his sister's death, because she had broken away from him. I could see the remorse and guilt in his eyes. He never talked about his feelings, but I could see pain and the heavy burden he carried. Von internalized and suppressed his feelings, but I knew there was a hole in his heart. Von and Tee bonded even closer as siblings, and I am sure it was because they shared a common tragic loss. Von tried so hard to be the strong shoulder for Tee and me. This was mind blowing for all of us to process. My only salvation was my relationship with God and my two children who gave me the strength day to day to manage the pain.

Believe me, the devil (the accuser) whispered in my ears, "You came out of the streets, got off drugs, and changed your life. Why did God let this happen to you? And right in front of the sanctuary where you worshiped!" He reminded me that when I returned to church, I had to relive the moments of this tragedy. At that moment, I was not sure how I was going to manage returning to the scene of the accident, but I knew God's grace was sufficient. I continued to seek answers from God about why this happened and why Yolanda had to die. I wanted to know if I had sinned against God to cause this thing to happen. I knew my God was a just and faithful God, so I examine myself for the cause of my loss. I went through one of those Job moments. The Word of God said during Job's afflictions, after the loss of his children, his servants, and his prosperity, he did not charge God foolishly.

Then Job arose, and rent his mantle, and shaved his head, and fell
down upon the ground, and worshipped, and said, Naked came I out
of my mother's womb, and naked shall I return thither: the LORD gave,
and the LORD hath taken away; blessed be the name of the LORD.
In all this Job sinned not, nor charged God foolishly.
(Job 1:20–22 KJV)

It was challenging for me to bounce back, but like the servant Job, I did
not charge God foolishly. Yolanda's dad was still a fugitive after breaking
out of prison. During the time of Yolanda's death, I was still in school
pursuing a degree in psychology. The preschool Yolanda was attending on
the college campus also provided emotional and monetary support. The
following Saturday after her death our pastor officiated the homegoing
services. It was a homegoing service but there was mush sadness, especially
for Tee and Von. The accident made it into the local newspaper. I always
had someone from my church family at my apartment comforting me and
helping me with my children. There was my god sister, Audrey who stayed
at my house for emotional support, helping with cleaning and caring for
Tee and Von. For a week after burying Yolanda, I stayed home praying
and seeking the face of God. The following Sunday, I decided I was going
to church to praise God. When I got there, the spirit of the Lord gave me
the grace to walk on the street where my daughter had died and enter our
church. Everyone's eyes fastened on me, expecting me to have an emotional
breakdown, "But God!" I rose to testify. As I was up praising God and
testifying, the Holy Spirit moved me to minister to the unsaved souls in the
house, encouraging them to give their lives to God before death overtook
them. My pastor gave me the permission to flow in the spirit. When I
finished testifying, about eight souls came to the altar to accept Christ as
their Savior. We danced and praised God! Seeing the souls coming to God
really blessed me even though I was still grieving the loss of my daughter.
I remember one of them was the pastor's daughter, who had rededicated
her life to God. My pain was navigating me into my divine purpose. I
worshiped God for using my testimony for the glory of God.

CHAPTER 10

....

When the Consequences of My Past Arrested Me

THE FOLLOWING WEEK, AFTER HAVING SUCH A HIGH TIME IN CHURCH, I faced another unexpected test. It was the unsettled legal matters related to my parole violation. It was a Monday afternoon, and I was resting. My god sister, Audrey, was at my apartment with me when there was a knock on my door. She answered the door. I heard a male voice asking her, "Is Mrs. Christine Byndon here?"

She responded, "Yes, sir." I went to the door, and this gentleman identified himself as a detective and said that he had a warrant for my arrest for parole violation. I was still grieving the death of my daughter, and I could not believe this was happening. After three years of my transformation, serving my God, being in church, reconciling with my family, and enjoying my freedom, the devil came to lock me up again! I had forgotten about my parole violation and had no idea they were looking for me. The detective said the court was able to locate me by the article in the newspaper about my daughter's accident. He was dress in plain clothes, and he said he was not going to place handcuffs on me so the neighbors would not know what was going on. He sympathized with me on the loss of my daughter and offered his condolences. He was very polite and sensitive to my situation.

I looked at Audrey and asked her to please call my parents and take care of my children when they came home from school. I willingly walked out with the detective and got into the back seat of his car. He took me downtown for booking and processing for confinement. All this time, I had been walking downtown and all over the city, and they claimed they could not find me. The glory of God covered me to the point they did not recognize me. I am a living witness that if any man be in Christ, he becomes a new creature. God made me brand-new in the spirit.

Therefore, if any man be in Christ, he is a new creature:
old things are passed away; behold, all things are become new.
(2 Corinthians 5:17 KJV)

God transformed me by His supernatural power, and I thank God for the blood of my Lord Jesus Christ. The glory of God had hidden me from my enemies. Glory to God! Hallelujah! The detective took me on the lower floor in the courthouse. They read me my rights and charged me for parole violation.

An unidentified officer said, "You are on your way back to prison to serve the rest of your six years because you violate your parole." I did not respond because I was too busy praying and thinking about my children. They fingerprinted me, patted me down, and gave me my new clothing, an orange outfit. I heard a couple of the prisoners saying, "That's Christine!" They were ladies who remembered me from the streets, but they also knew I was now in the church serving God. My testimony had preceded me by the time I went to jail. Guards were giving me their condolences for the loss of my daughter. When the jailer locked me in, I fell on my knees and began to pray. I prayed aloud, praising God until the other inmates began praying and praising God with me. While in jail, I met a young lady who was preparing to leave for confinement to prison after her conviction of murder. I took advantage of an opportunity to minister unto her about Salvation and prayed with her.

For we know that all things work together
for good to them that love God,
to them who are the called according to his purpose.
(Romans 8:28 KJV)

I was not sure of my outcome, but my trust was in God, and I had to trust the process. If it were in God's divine plan for me to return to prison, I made up my mind that while there, I would be a witness for Christ. While I was in jail, I heard from someone that my church family had gathered in the sanctuary, fervently and passionately crying out to God for my release. My first night in jail was peaceful. I was convinced that God was going to intervene, and things were going to work out to my favor. God was going to get all the glory!

Early the next morning one of the jailers brought my breakfast. The jailer made it known that there was discussion about me praying. That morning, I expected a visit from my mother, and I was excited about seeing her. I wanted to know how my children were doing. Ladies in my jail block began to ask me to pray for them. I allowed the Lord to use me to witness to a couple of ladies that was feeling hopeless about their future. I know the Lord had planted good seeds in their hearts. Later in the day, the jailer called my name and informed me I had a visitor. I was so excited to see my mom and my sister Evelyn. Mom told me about a gentleman she had met on the elevator. My mom never met a stranger without talking about God. She engaged him in a conversation by telling him she was on her way to see her daughter. He asked her, "What is your daughter's name?" Mom gave him my name, and he introduced himself as my parole officer. He told her that he was in the process of seeing if they would release me from jail.

Evelyn was still taking the death of Yolanda extremely hard. She looked at me through the secure window and said to me, "If your God brings you out of this, I'll get saved!"

I looked at her and said, "You'd better get ready to get saved because God is going to bring me out of this!"

Mom said, "Chris, I saw you in a vision last night, and you came into my bedroom. I said to you, 'Christine! What are you doing here; how did you get out?' It was so real; God was letting me know that you were coming home." I was excited about the confirmation because I knew if my mom said it, then it was so! The power of my mother's prayer and the anointing upon my mom was still at work! I started praising God and expecting to be release. I told my mom I had already committed to God if it is in His will for me to go back to prison, I would go as a born-again believer preaching His Word. I had such a commitment in my heart to serve God, and nothing was going to separate me from Him. Sometimes we do not understand the ways of God and will never get the answers to our whys, but I had to trust God even when I did not understand His divine purpose. I had to recall and meditate on His Word.

> There hath no temptation taken you but such as is common to man:
> but God is faithful, who will not suffer you to be tempted
> above that ye are able; but will with the temptation also
> make a way to escape, that ye may be able to bear it.
> (1 Corinthians 10:13 KJV)

CHAPTER 11

The Angel of the Lord Opened My Jail Door

I RETURNED TO MY JAIL CELL AFTER MY VISIT WITH MOM AND MY SISTER with excitement and a Paul and Silas praise, as recorded in Acts 16:25 (KJV). "And at midnight Paul and Silas prayed, and sang praises unto God: and the prisoners heard them." Everyone in the cell block could hear me praising God!

Before I could sit on my bed, I was call for another visit. It was a gentleman who identified himself as my parole officer. He said, "Hello, my name is Mr. Glenn Greene. I am assigned as your parole officer." He informed me that he had met my mother on the elevator as he was coming up to see me. He said, "You must be a very special person and love by many, because my phone hasn't stopped ringing off the hook since you've been in here." He said that he has received phone calls testifying about my character and integrity. He said, "Several people have recommended for the parole board to release you from jail. I received a phone call from a prominent person within the community requesting the parole board to reconsider the state decision to revoke your parole, because you are a changed person and influential individual within the community. You will be released out of here today as soon as I get your paperwork completed and signed by my supervisor."

I looked at him with tears in my eyes and responded, "Thank you, sir!" I returned to my jail cell rejoicing and praising God, and I believe every inmate could hear me. The ladies on my cell block were praising God for me and asking me to pray for them. I spent one night and a day in jail. When I got home, I was glad to see my children, and they were glad to see me. My god sister remained at the apartment with my children until I returned home. She made sure they had a satisfying meal, helped them with their homework, and she kept them entertained. The word spread to my church family that their prayers were answer and I was home. Church members were calling and stopping by my apartment to visit me. They all came with encouraging words and praising God with me. I was still grieving the loss of my baby, but everyone was doing everything in their power to embrace and comfort my children and me.

I received a letter with a phone number from Frog requesting I call him. I knew he was grieving the loss of our daughter too, and he had regrets that he was not able to attend her funeral. Yolanda was his only child. I telephoned him the next day out of respect and to process feelings concerning our daughter's death. I took that opportunity to witness Christ to him and encouraged Frog to give his life to God. It was a short conversation, and I kept it spiritual. He was still running and hiding from the police. At the end of our phone conversation, I said, "Frog, you need to turn your life over to God! You need to get saved!"

About a month later, I received a phone call from someone who said he was calling from New York to tell me that Frog was dead. I asked, "How did he die?" The person informed me that Frog had jumped out a high elevated building and committed suicide. That report was hard for me to believe until his uncle called me to confirm it.

After my release from jail, I spent all my time with my children. There were five days before the church doors would be open. Sunday could not come quick enough because I was ready to attend church and get with the saints to praise God. My testimony was, "God has done it again!" His grace and mercies had sustained me and proven my commitment to Him before the unbelievers.

I was glad when they said to me,
"Let us go to the house of the LORD."
(Psalm 122:1 NLT)

The church was full, and the praise was on fire! I came in with a shout and a praise. We shouted and ran up and down the aisles in victory for what God has done. The Spirit of God was so heavy that our pastor could not preach. Pastor allowed the Spirit of God to move freely upon His people. Just before the church service ended, my sister Evelyn walked in the church. Her intention was to run in and head back out after picking up money from one of our sisters. The outpouring of the anointing saturated the entire atmosphere. The Spirit of God fell upon Evelyn as she was on her way out of the door. Evelyn began to cry out and the spirit of God drew her to the altar with her hands up and tears falling down her face, and I heard her asking God to save her. Praise God! It was a divine setup. What a mighty outpouring of the Holy Ghost! This was the same sister who had visited me while I was in jail and said, "If your God brings you out of this, I will get saved!" Glory to God!

Romans 8:28 (KJV) states, "And we know that all things work together for good to them that love God, to them who are the called according to his purpose." As a result of my daughter's transition to heaven and my endurance of suffering, lost souls came to Christ.

Romans 8:18 (KJV) states, "For I reckon that the sufferings of this present time are not worthy to be compared with the glory which shall be revealed in us."

The sufferings I had to endure was challenging, but worth the glory we encountered that day and seeing Evelyn giving her life to God! After that encounter I witnessed God using her mightily as she continues to develop her relationship with Him. God called Evelyn into ministry, and into her divine assignment to pastor the church established by our mother.

What the enemy meant for bad, God turned it for my good and for the good of those that gave their lives to God. The following week, I received another unexpected blessing that came through the mail. I received a legal document from my parole officer stating that my parole status had been discontinue, and all my citizen rights reinstated. I did not know for the three years of my acceptance of salvation that I had lost certain privileges as a citizen because of my felony. God restored to me everything the devil took away from me and compensated me with increase. Hallelujah! Glory to God! I know it was the grace of God that brought me through everything I had to endure. After the dust settled during this challenging time, I still had my testimony and maintained my commitment to God.

CHAPTER 12

My Breaking Point

ABOUT A MONTH AFTER BURYING YOLANDA, I ATTEMPTED TO BRING normalcy to my life and the lives of my children. I received ten thousand dollars from my life insurance policy, not to mention financial blessings from others. I continued to attend church, house prayer meetings, and other church events. I returned to school to pursue my college degree. While I was studying in the library on my first day back, I had an emotional breakdown and could not control the tears. I had to leave school that day. That breakdown was evidence that I was still grieving; I thought I was good, but I repressed my pain. I requested a short leave of absence before returning to school. The university was empathetic and was patient with me until I gained more emotional stability. I tried so hard to be super spiritual, preventing myself from going through the grieving process. It was the breakdown at school that awakened me to the reality that I needed to stop, exhale, and allow myself to feel my pain.

When I exhaled, it was like a levy had broken, and the rushing water was unstoppable. My pain was so overwhelming, I could not begin to imagine the effect this tragic accident had on Tee and Von. I thought taking them to church would heal them and interacting with their friends would redirect their focus on happy moments. Church was my solution for everything. Going to church was helpful, but it did not take away all our pain. I thank God for Mom, who filled in the void for me in taking care of Von and Tee. My younger sister, who was around the same age as Von, cared for them as if they were siblings. They shared their pain and tears together. Also, I thank God for Gary visiting and spending time with us. Gary was a blessing in supporting and providing for both Von and Tee. Gary would make sure Tee had all she needed for school and would buy Christmas for both Tee and Von. In fact, he would take Tee to his hometown for summer vacations. It was a blessing to have his support. He was a responsible parent and took care of his daughter.

God continued to connect me with people who invested in my efforts to enhance my spiritual and personal growth. A community resource, the Vocational Rehabilitation Services, offered me educational opportunities and special financial assistance through a federal grant. This grant was specifically for those released from prison on felony crime. After a couple of weeks, I was able to return to college to complete my degree. I continued to have challenging days, but God strengthened me day by day. I finally graduated with a Bachelor of Science in psychology, and I remained on the dean's list throughout my junior and senior years. I was so grateful to God for keeping my mind focused enough to accomplish my goals. I desired to work in the field of substance abuse counseling. Because God had delivered me from drug addiction, I wanted to give back to other individuals suffering from addiction. When I received my diploma, I very proudly presented it to my mother as a means of making amends for all the disappointments I had caused her. Mom was so proud of me and my accomplishments.

My faith continued to grow in Christ, and my heart was full of gratitude. The gratitude was obvious, even when I shared my testimony, it would be lengthy. My pastor would give me permission to allow God to speak through me. People would tell me that the calling of preaching was upon me. I began to accept the call to ministry, but my pastor had to affirm my calling. I confided in my pastor that I felt the calling of ministry of preaching upon my life. About five years after receiving Christ, the late Bishop Townsend affirmed and ordained me as a minister. I knew I still had unsolved emotional issues I had not dealt with, so I did not feel I was ready to step into the ministry quite yet. I masked and tried to minimize the pain and anger that was in my heart because of the loss of my daughter. I camouflaged my humanity by being spiritual and denying my weakness. My godmother, Momma Lottie, said to me, "Whatever areas you are short in, when you tell God yes, the ministry will put a demand on you to come up!"

I wanted people to perceived me as a strong Christian. People thought

I was managing my grief well, but I really was suppressing and walking in a state of denial. I struggled with loneliness. I just wanted companionship, not sex. I knew my demons and my weaknesses, so I would do everything to abstain from any temptation. I recalled meeting a male friend who told me I needed to learn to have male friends without assuming a man wanted to be intimate with me. I could not take any chances in compromising my testimony. I was too vulnerable to entertain a meaningful relationship with the other sex. All I knew was unhealthy relationships with the men I knew from the streets. It was always conditional or codependency, which set me up for abuse or used as invaluable property. Those old, seasoned mothers kept me covered with their firm teaching and standards. I appreciated the grace of God sustaining me through my growing process.

I continued to seek God's face through prayer and fasting as I prepared myself for the day of my official sermon. The day came for me to stand before the people to minister, and I was feeling anxious. My family and friends traveled near and far, and visitors from other churches were in attendance. My prayer partners, who were also my mentors were always present to encourage and support me. My message was the same as those old Pentecostal sermons, "Living Holy" and crucifying the flesh. My pastor who was my spiritual father was so proud of me and gave me his blessings. My mom was delighted to see her heart's desire come to fruition. The Lord gave me a holy boldness. I would preach forcefully and attack any demonic forces that I struggled with prior to accepting Christ, especially the spirit of fornication and addiction. As I reflected on the message of my ministry it was more on the judgment of God than His grace and love because that was the message throughout my upbringing years.

In the year 2001, my pastor and the Bishop's Board ordain me as an evangelist within our church's organization, and soon the board affirmed my calling. My pastor gave his blessings and kept me covered while serving under his leadership. Serving my local church took priority over any other engagements. During my time of evangelizing, there was a turning point in the lives of my children because ministry took time away from my presence at home. I would bring them to church with me, but we did not have that quality family time. My life was church and ministry! I became so spiritually minded, trying to fix everyone else and ministering to everyone else's children, but I neglected my own children and myself. There was a great demand for me to preach revivals throughout North Carolina and other states. I saw so many souls saved, folks delivered from addictions, and people set free from demonic forces and healed. My mindset was doing whatever I could do to serve others in any capacity I could.

By this time, I was working in the professional field as a certified substance abuse therapist. God used my profession to help people who suffered from drug addiction and their children who struggled from the effects of addiction. My career as an addiction specialist was also my ministry to help these ladies fight their demons. Between ministry and working, I really failed in addressing my emotions and mental state. I put on this façade that I was so spiritual and strong, but I was lonely and trying to privately fight my own demons. I stayed on the defense when it came to men that wanted to date me, whether they were in the church or unchurched. I refused to entertain anything that would arouse lustful desires. Even throughout my evangelistic ministry, I would attack sexual sins hard because that was one of my strongholds. I had been celibate for ten years, until one Friday night when I put myself in a compromising position that led me to commit fornication. It was the sin I feared the most because lust was my stronghold before accepting Christ as my Savior. I remembered afterward crying so intensively with sorrow and broken heart because I had failed God. I cried throughout the night, and sleep left my eyes. Going to sleep without confessing this sin was not an option for me.

It was extremely late in the night, but I picked up the phone and called my mother's number. She answered, but I could barely speak from crying. Mom woke up out of her sleep and asked, "What's wrong, Chris?"

I finally got the words out of my mouth and confessed, "Mom! I had a fall tonight!" I was crying so hard and loud that I could barely hear her response. I could not believe I had fallen into this sin of fornication. I could not believe that I had opened that door of lust that compromised my testimony after being celibate for ten years.

I was devastated, but my mother was so compassionate as she ministered to my spirit. She said, "Chris, it will be all right. God has already forgiven you by the words of your confession right now! I can hear the sorrow and the hurt in your voice because you feel you have let God down!"

I was crying and repeatedly saying, "I failed God!" I was so mad at myself for resisting the warning of the Holy Spirit. The devil came to me during one of the most vulnerable, darkest, and loneliest times of my life since becoming a believer. The devil had caught me off guard!

> Be sober, be vigilant; because your adversary the devil,
> as a roaring lion, walketh about, seeking whom he may devour.
> (1 Peter 5:8 KJV)

> Wherefore let him that thinketh he standeth take heed lest he fall.
> (1 Corinthians 10:12 KJV)

It was only the grace of God that sustained and conditioned me throughout all my temptations and life challenges. I had to acknowledge that I was who I was, and I was able to withstand the works of the devil by the power of God, only by the grace of God! None of us have any righteousness of our own; it is only the righteousness of God through the blood of our Lord, Savior Jesus Christ, which makes us righteous before the throne of God. I prayed and fasted, pleading with God to totally restore me. I did not realize just how vulnerable I had become to falling into fornication. I thank God for new mercies every morning, and for the blood of Jesus Christ shed on Calvary that covers all our unrighteousness and gives us access to the throne of God.

My mother is a prayer warrior and a demon chaser. She prayed strategically against the assignment of demonic forces that came with the intent to cause me to abort my ministry. Mom's prayer was with authority, power and heavy anointed until I could feel the love of God healing my heart, a spirit of healing came over me, and I felt lifted in my spirit. I do not remember what time I drifted off to sleep, but it was a peaceful rest. When I woke up the next morning, I was still feeling remorseful. I began to think of the possibility of being pregnant and pleaded with God not to allow this thing to come upon me. Even though I did not deserve anything but death and hell, I did not want the consequence of my sin to mark my ministry. The devil only keeps one focused on the gratification of a thing, but then one fails to consider the long-term effects on generations to come. I felt like I was under a dark cloud, but I rose with praise because God did not allow death to overtake me during my sin. He gave me a second chance!

I reconnected with my mom later that day and she greeted me with a hug and compassion. I felt like I was in the arms of God when she embraced me. She ministered to me, not only to my spirit but from a human perspective as well. Even though I had the assurance God forgave me and felt restored, I still struggled with self-forgiveness. I silenced myself for a couple of months by refusing to accept any preaching engagements. I wanted to make sure I was not pregnant. I thanked my God I was negative for a sexually transmitted disease. My mother continued to minister to my spirit and encouraged me to keep the faith. God was using Mom more prophetically, and her ministry expanded. She was evangelizing and traveling to do revivals. Later, God promoted my mother in her kingdom assignment as a pastor. She opened her first church in a storefront building. I eventually joined her ministry to help her and further my spiritual growth. I thank God for grace and Mercy, and that He spared me from the shame of my sin: I was not pregnant.

I continued to walk in my divine assignment, preaching and teaching the Word of God. My children and I moved to a prominent neighborhood and into our very first house. Between churches, preaching revivals, and going to work, I am sure my children suffered from a lack of quality time with me. I was working out of town in Pinehurst, North Carolina, as a substance abuse therapist. Von and Tee began misbehaving and skipping school. Von started breaking house rules, coming in past his curfew, getting in trouble at school and getting failing grades; therefore, his grades dropped. At the age of fifteen, Tee began to hang out with a crowd of which I strongly disapproved. There were other challenges in her life that damaged and inflicted pain upon her and complicated our mother-daughter relationship. I remember Tee saying to me, "Mom, I need you to be my mom, not a preacher or a counselor!" I did not realize that I was failing her as a mother. She made it known that I was out of touch with her feelings as her mother. I allowed issues outside the home to have my attention, rather than focusing on my children's needs. I was working to save everyone else's family but neglecting my own. That statement from Tee really opened my eyes and I heard her loud and clear. I understood her resentment because I had the same feelings growing up. I did not realize how deep and how damaged she was emotionally and mentally.

Von was struggling also. Gary was there for Tee, but I tried to fill the gap Von was experiencing by not having a father in his life. During this troublesome time of my relationship with my children, Tee became pregnant at the age of fifteen. I did not manage my feelings well concerning her pregnancy, and it damaged her even more. My mother stepped in for support, and Tee moved in with her. I thank God for my mother, who was my hero, my strength, and my prayer warrior. She was always there to encourage me no matter what my challenge was. My mother saw Tee through her high school prom and her high school graduation. I was so proud of Tee, and I regret not attending because of our conflicts. I remembered seeing her prom pictures and Mom had her dressed so beautifully. She had her hair cut in a classy style. My pretty little girl had grown into a beautiful young lady. Tee always had a special bond with her grandmother than she did with me. I am sure it was because her grandmother had always been there during her most challenging times in life. Mom walked Tee through her pregnancy and was there when she birthed her son, Pierre. I thank God also for my youngest sister, Erika, who was there for Tee and Von as a sister and a friend. She was there for Tee through her pain of anguish.

I would go out of my way trying to make amends by buying material things to bring healing in our relationship. I love my children very much and always prayed and trusted God to bring healing in our relationship, especially with Tee. Von was failing school because of his grades and lack of attendance. He feared he would fail his senior year, so Von was talking to a marine recruiter without my knowledge. He felt his only option was to join the military. During this time, I suffered and struggled in silence. No one knew my struggles and pain; I was losing my balance in life. I wore a mask even when I preached, watching others getting their deliverance, converted, and healed.

I tried to juggle everything that was coming upon me, I felt the pressure of life and felt overburden spiritually and emotionally. The desire for companionship was getting strong, and I struggled with loneliness. I also experienced warfare in my mind. I can testify what the Apostle Paul said in Romans 7:16–18 (NIV), "And if I do what I do not want to do, I agree that the law is good. As it is, it is no longer I myself who do it, but it is sin living in me. For I know that good itself does not dwell in me, that is, in my sinful nature. For I have the desire to do what is good, but I cannot carry it out."

Despite all the struggles in my flesh during my spiritual journey, I was determined not to return into the slavery of sin, and I would not be a hypocrite. I learned to defeat the devil's strategy of temptation by exposing his tactics through open confession, seeking wisdom from my mother or a spiritual mother. I prayed, fasted, and remained in the Word of God continuously to withstand against the wiles of the devil, as recorded in the Word of God: "Put on the whole armour of God, that ye may be able to stand against the wiles of the devil" (Ephesians 6:11 KJV).

I thank God for not giving up on me. I love what the Word says in Proverbs 24:16 (KJV), "For a just man falleth seven times, and riseth up again: but the wicked shall fall into mischief." When we are sincere about our relationship with God, He will strengthen and empower us to overcome. I continued to preach, ministering hope, love, and peace to the troubled mind. God was getting all the glory during my preaching engagements. The prophetic anointing and the spirit of discernment were in operation while ministering, but I needed a healing within me.

One night while praying, I felt a radical praise that overtook me, and I began warring in the spirit until God gave me an inward breakthrough. The anointing bound up the "strong man" that had yoked me for about three months with fleshy desires. The grace of God is sufficient, and it helped me overcome and conquer every demon assigned to bind me and keep me from fulfilling my divine assignment. I felt whole again and liberated from demonic oppression. After God restored my spirit, I experienced a supernatural manifestation of His power at work during revival services. I witnessed people deliver from strongholds, people filled with the Holy Ghost as evidenced by speaking in tongues, and souls converted. There began to be a demand for the ministry. I gained favor and love throughout the church community.

The revival engagements increased but I sought the permission of my pastor before accepting. I thought I was operating in a loving and humble fashion as I served God's people. In honoring my spiritual father, late Bishop Townsend, he requested I do a revival at my home church. One night after service, one of the church mothers, Mother Crecy, came up behind me and asked to speak to me privately. I knew that she was going to say something prophetic or give me an encouraging word, but it was a word of rebuke. She said in a soft tone, "Evangelist Byndon, I don't mean any harm, but God told me to tell you that you need to humble yourself." I was not expecting that rebuke from her, especially after God had used me so mightily that night. I did not think I had a prideful spirit. I became offended and rejected her rebuke. I went home and told my mom what she had said.

My mom did not deny it or defend it, but she said to me, "Well, you need to pray about it." My first impression of this church mother's rebuke was only because I had makeup on my face, with rings on my fingers and gold necklaces hanging from my neck. I was dress fashionable. I really had to get beyond my flesh and consider Mother Crecy was right: the spirit of pride had overtaken me. Before ending the revival, I went to that church mother to repent and confess that she was right. After that rebuke, I repented to God. God led me to remove pieces of my jewelry, especially when preaching, so it would not be a distraction or a hindrance to reach when I preached. I had to admit I was trying to look good outwardly so men would see me, rather than putting the light on God. Every month, I received calls to do revivals within the city and surrounding areas, not to mention women's conferences. Walking in my divine assignment and bringing souls into the kingdom of God was my passion, primarily because through the power of God, souls came into the kingdom of the God.

CHAPTER 13

"Momma, Don't Go to Church Tonight"

MY ONLY SON DECIDED TO JOIN THE MARINE CORPS AFTER HIS HIGH school graduation. He preferred I called him Travis after graduation and joining the marine corps. I was proud that he wanted to serve our country, but I did not want him to join the marines. I had heard that the marine corps was the most challenging branch of the military, and I was not sure Travis could endure the pressure of their training. I assumed this was normal as a mom being afraid and having reservations about her child going into the military. I remember on a Saturday morning I drove him to a location to catch the van as scheduled to transport the guys to boot camp. It was a white twelve-passenger van. There were young white and men of color already inside. As I watched him take his bags out of the car and load them into the van, reality hit me that my son was leaving me. My eyes filled with tears, but I tried hard to hide them from him. As he came to kiss me and say goodbye, the tears streamed down my face. Travis kept a straight face without responding to my emotions. I was proud of him but sad at the same time. I had to gather myself together because I did not want him to leave preoccupied with my sadness. I regained my composure and told him how proud I was that he wanted to serve our country. I prayed with him and told him to call me as soon as he could.

I waited a couple of weeks for his call but kept him in my prayers daily. After a couple of months, Travis called to tell me that he had successfully completed the boot camp training. I remembered that phone call from him was full of excitement as he said, "Momma, I made it! I passed the boot camp training!" He gave me the date of his graduation. He was excited about the day of being affirm as a marine at Camp Lejeune. I felt elated and proud to have a son as a marine. My parents, sisters and brother traveled with me to Camp Lejeune. When I got on the base, I saw my son dressed in his marine corps uniform. He was standing so tall with a big smile when he saw us. He stood tall as a proud US Marine, ready to serve his country. I must say my son's whole disposition, mindset, attitude, and even his conversation was at another level of maturity. His military graduation was during the time of Operation Desert Storm, and he was already talking about going to war for our country.

After Travis received his duties and settled in his company, he would call me as often as he could. I could tell in his voice that he was experiencing challenges with his sergeant. but I kept speaking words of encouragement to him. About a month later, Travis was able to have a weekend pass to come home. My dad sends him a bus pass to travel home. That weekend I was at the bus station ahead of time, waiting for him. He looked so good as he stepped off that bus fully dressed in his marine uniform. Travis would visit home at least twice monthly. Sometimes he would call to tell me that he was assign extra duty, which prohibited him from coming home. He had a circle of friends from his company who would come home with him. I would plan a special meal for him each time. He would take military friends around town to meet his neighborhood friends. As time progressed, during visiting at home, I could tell that he was becoming homesick. It would get harder and harder for him to prepare to leave, waiting until the very last minute. He would verbalize how he wished he could stay home a little longer, but he always returned to base when ordered. I did not know what kinds of challenges he faced while in the marines, and he never shared any with me. I felt helpless because I wanted to resolve whatever the problem was.

It was getting close to a year that Travis had served in the marines, and he planned to come home that weekend to celebrate with family. The week before, Travis had driven home to visit family. He spends quality time with his one-year-old nephew, Pierre. That Saturday, the weekend of his visit Travis took Pierre to the mall and bought him an expensive pair of tennis shoes. When he returned home, I asked him, "Why did you spend that much money on tennis shoes for a baby?"

He said, "That's my nephew, and I'm going to get him the best!" When it was time for him to return to Camp Lejeune, he took Tee and his nephew with him to spend more time with them. His plan was to bring them back the following weekend. Tee and I were still at odds with each other, and she was living with her boyfriend. Travis attempted to be a mediator to assist in reconciling our relationship. He loved his sister and had a special love for his nephew. He called me later in the week to confirm that he would be coming home that weekend to celebrate his year as a marine. We were so excited and ready to celebrate with him. His granddad, my dad, was especially happy because Travis had given him his heart's desire by joining the military. Travis had a special bond with his grandmother, my mother. He would call her his Teddy Bear. My son was an affectionate loving boy, and he did not have any problem demonstrate affection to any of us, through hugs and kisses, especially Grandma and aunties.

The weekend of his one-year celebration being a marine came to a tragic ending on the next day, that Sunday evening. Sunday evening, we had our last conversation before his death. I was preparing to go to church for a preaching engagement, and he was preparing to return to Camp Lejeune. As I was dressing for church, Travis said to me, "Momma, don't go to church tonight!" There was something different about how he said those words; it was as if a little boy was crying out in desperation for his momma to stay with him. I hugged him and said, "Boy, I can't cancel this service now; I am expected to be there within a couple of hours." That was Travis's last request of me: "Momma don't go to church tonight!" Those are the last words I clearly remembered my nineteen-year-old son saying to me. I suggested he request an emergency leave when he returns to Camp Lejeune for a couple of days in the following week, because I had medical concerns. I told him we could spend time together and talk then. He agreed to do so, but it was obvious that he was not pleased with delaying our talk. I hugged him and told him I loved him and would see him when he returned, and I left for church.

I had one of my spiritual daughters assisting me in ministry that night; her name was Sylvia. When we arrived at the church, there was a good crowd there, and the presence of God filled the house. I will never forget the title of my sermon, "I'm Going through, but I'm Coming Out with More than What I Had." My subject came from the Book of Job. I did not realize at that time that my theme was a prophetic word for me. I was prophesying to myself and did not even know it. We all received a blessing through the Word of God as I ministered His Message. I was at my home church, with my spiritual father, the late Bishop William Townsend, fulfilling my God-given assignment. I later found out during the exact time I was preaching my sermon, my son was a victim involved in a serious car accident outside of town, near Newton Grove. While preaching I had no idea Travis was in an accident. While I was preaching, a heavy spirit came over me, and I said to the congregation that I felt a familiar spirit. I could not put my finger on what I was feeling, but it was burdensome. After church, I asked Sylvia to pull into a services station so I could put gas in the car. As we both stood at the gas pump, I said to her, "This is a familiar feeling. I felt this heaviness just before my three-year-old daughter died."

She replied, "Really, Evangelist Byndon!" She drove me home and said goodbye. When I got into the house, I could barely undress myself because of the heavy feeling in my spirit. I fell on the bed to rest when a friend called me. I tried to explain what I was feeling but was unable, so I cut the conversation short. I fell on my knees trying to pray but could not find the words. The Holy Spirit came over me, and I began to speak in my heavenly language. The Holy Spirit interceded on my behalf. For the Word of God says, "Likewise the Spirit also helpeth our infirmities: for we know not what we should pray for as we ought: but the Spirit itself maketh intercession for us with groanings which cannot be uttered" (Romans 8:26 KJV).

I got up from the floor after praying and went to the bed in quietness. Then my phone rang. The lady on the other end of the phone asked, "Is this Mrs. Christine Byndon?" I said yes. She said, "I am calling from Highsmith Hospital, and we need you to come to the hospital. Your son was in an accident."

I became hysterical and asked, "Is he okay?"

The nurse replied, "Ma'am, do you have anyone to drive you here? We need you to come as soon as you can."

I did not think about calling anyone at the time, so I drove myself. All the way to the hospital, I repeatedly told myself, "My son is all right." It kept coming to me that Travis was dead. I started rebuking what I thought was the devil's report. I kept saying, "Devil, you're a liar! My son is not dead!" All the time, it was God trying to prepare me for what I was about to face.

I ran into the emergency room and requested to see my son, Travis Byndon. A nurse came from the back to lead me into a small room. I waited all alone for the doctor to come speak to me. The doctor finally came in a couple minutes later, looked at me, and said, "Ma'am, I'm sorry, but we could not save your son."

I screamed with tears of despair. I fell to the floor, saying, "No! No! Not my son! Not Travis!" I told the doctor I wanted to see my baby. I kept saying to the doctor, "No! Not my baby!" I knocked medical utensils off the table and cried uncontrollably. I was alone with the doctor and nurse, who tried to console me. The doctor asked if I wanted to call anyone. I said, "Yes, my mom!" I called Mom bellowing but trying to catch my breath, and the nurse stood by my side.

Mom said, "What's wrong, Chris?"

I said to her, "Mom, Travis is dead!"

Mom said in shock, "No! No! No Chris!"

I heard Dad say to her, "What's wrong, Ruth?"

She said, "Von is dead!" Mom went into shock. Dad took the phone, and I told him where I was. I felt like my heart had left my body.

The only one I could think to call next was my prayer partner and best friend Vertell. I spoke to her and Reverend Godbolt and informed them about the accident. I said, "I don't think I am going to make it through this one!" I could barely get the words out because I was crying so violently. Being at that hospital by myself was like being on an isolated island with no hope, trapped in a whirlwind taking me to a place of no return. I kept asking the doctor if I could see my son, but the doctor thought it would be best for me to wait for family support. I waited anxiously to see him.

Mom and Dad finally came, and I fell in my mother's arms, weeping. Word got around to my family and to my daughter. They all arrived at the hospital. Tee was with her boyfriend but was on her way to the hospital. I was anxious and had to go in immediately to see Travis. I could not wait another minute! When I entered the room, I saw my son's body on the bed as if Travis was sleep. I placed my head on his chest and started crying and calling his name. "Travis! Travis! My baby!" I could smell the sweat from his body, from fighting death. The doctor said he had died from multiple injuries, but the main injury was a broken neck. The car flipped and ejected Travis through the back window of the car. Travis was not wearing a seatbelt at the time of the accident. Tee entered the hospital with Pierre, my grandson, in her arms, crying in disbelief that her brother was dead.

Everyone was heartbroken with the passing of Travis. I kept asking God, "Why? Why did you take my son?" I started trying to reason with God as to why this had happened to me. I asked God, "Am I being punished for the times I failed you?" I continued throughout that night trying to understand why this happened, especially on a night I was preaching and ministering. It did not make sense to me. It was a sleepless night for me, and I could not find any comfort, even with my family surrounding me.

The next day, there was a knock at the front door. It was a marine officer coming to pay his condolences and informing me of Travis's insurance benefits that I would receive. He gave me a check for the initial arrangements. He then told me that the base chaplain thought it important for me to know that Travis was attending church services while on post, and he was developing a relationship with God. That blessed my heart to hear Travis was seeking God and attending church. I remembered times having conversations with Travis about repentance and accepting Christ in his life. He knew about the love of God and how to pray.

Travis always played the role of hero for Tee and me. That was the reason he had joined the military: to make a career for himself and take care of us, including his nephew, Pierre.

As I reflect, it was not easy being a single parent, working full time, and fulfilling my obligations to ministry. I was grateful to have Christ as Savior and Lord of my life during this time. Serving Christ brought sanity back into my life and restored custody rights of my children. There were so many blessings given to me after surrendering my life to God.

In retrospect, the weekend Tee and Travis spent together orchestrated by our all-knowing God, who knew this would be the last weekend they would have with each other on earth. It was an enjoyable and pleasant closure the family and I had with him before his death. At the beginning of Travis's home visit Saturday morning, he made his rounds with his friends. When he returned home that Saturday evening, Travis and I shared quality time laughing and talking, and our conversation took an unexpected turn. It was an unusual and unexpected moment because my son was opening his heart to me in a way that he never did. He began passionately sharing his love for me and expressing how proud he was of all my accomplishments. He even expressed gratitude for how I was able to raise him and his sisters as a single parent. He stood six feet and five inches and took me in his arms, holding me tightly, repeatedly expressing his love for me, and reassuring me that he was going to take care of his sister and me. He had this serious look on his face and looked me directly in my eyes with a deep stare I had never witnessed from him before. It was a special mother-son moment! Travis expressed his concerns about the conflicts Teresa, and I were having at that time, and he attempted to be the mediator. As we were concluding our chat, Travis took his conversation to another level as he pulled me closer and said, "Mom, I meant to tell you that I increased my insurance policy for you, and I got one for Aunt Rere" (who is Evelyn, my second oldest sister).

I pushed him away, lightly hit him on the shoulder, and said, "Boy, I don't want to hear about that!" He gave me a bear hug, and we started laughing. I chuckled with him but did not allow him to see how uncomfortable I felt by his conversation, especially talking about his life insurance policy. Travis needed a little more support and encouragement, and I am sure not having a father in his life was a contributive factor. Everyone that met Tee fell in love with her, and she was spoil by her father, grandmother, and aunties. People spoke often of her beauty and her beautiful hair. The next day, on Sunday morning I prepared breakfast for Travis and me. His time home was full of joy and special for the both of us. The phone continued to ring for Travis; it was his friends and a girlfriend in town. I was preparing for morning church service and had a preaching engagement later that evening. I left Travis at home preparing to return to Camp Lejeune. Tee had planned to return with Travis to spend more time with him. After returning from the morning service at church, I prepared a good dinner for us before his departure. I informed Travis of a letter I had received from my doctor expressing concerns about a mass found on my breast from an ultrasound. I shared with him my concern of having breast cancer. I was not aware at the time that Travis had a secret he wanted to share with me but did not share it after I told him about my medical concerns. It was getting closer to the time for me to leave to fulfill my preaching engagement. After having an enjoyable Saturday and Sunday morning, that Sunday evening ended in sorrow and unbelievable sadness. That Sunday evening my son died in a car accident! I recall the conversation and events prior to me leaving him as I prepared for church that evening as if it was yesterday.

Travis said to me, "Momma, don't go to church! Can you stay home until I leave?" It was so strange that he asked me to stay home and not go to church. Travis knew how committed I was to ministry, and I depended on church as my lifeline. I did not give it a second thought at the time because we had made plans for him to request an emergency leave to come back home the following week, so we could spend more time together. I am sure on his way back to Camp Lejeune; his thoughts focused on my medical issues and other personal issues. I found out after his death that he wanted to inform me that he had gotten someone pregnant. I kissed and hugged him farewell until he returned next week. Someone informed me that Travis went by his grandmother's house to talk with her on his way out, but she was not home. When I considered the urgency of what he was carrying on his heart, all I could think about was how burdened and troubled my son must have been as he was driving back to Camp Lejeune.

Traveling back to Camp Lejeune he died in a fatal accident. Travis lost control of the car as he was going around a curve, and thrown from the car through the back window, resulting in multiple injuries. Police report stated he did not have his seat belt on. I contacted the prison correctional center to inform his father of his death. The prison system allowed Slim to come to his funeral. Slim never had an opportunity to spend one day of free time with his son because of his confinement in prison for 120 years. This death was nothing like what I had experienced with my three-year-old daughter. It was harder, maybe because I had spent nineteen years with him.

I thank God that my children had no conscious remembrance of my years of struggling with addiction and my sinful lifestyle. They knew only what they heard from other people and from my testimony of how I had overcome my past. However, I wish I could have done things differently in raising my children. I would have spent more quality time with them. I raised them in a Christian home with Christian values. But in hindsight, there were times I felt like I neglected them. Yes, I take responsibility of mistakes I made, but those words my son spoke into my life was like a big eraser, removing all my failures as a mother and the times I was absent when they needed me the most. His words were a healing balm to my soul.

This reflection is so bittersweet! Reflecting on this moment and revisiting my sadness have stirred up so many painful memories. Yet I feel another level of healing taking place even as I am authoring my book.

I buried Travis on November 3rd, the same day of my deceased daughter's birthday. The day after burying Travis, my daughter continued to reside with her boyfriend. I felt as if I had experienced two losses that day: my son was dead, and my daughter Tee had left home. I grieved all by myself, but God never left me. My parents, my siblings, and my church family embraced me, and they sat with me every day. It took a long time for me to move into the healing process and accept what God had allowed. I simply could not wrap my mind around the reality that my son was dead. There were times I would be driving in from work and angrily ask the question, "Travis, why didn't you put on your seat belt?" I had to give myself time to heal and come to the realization that there was no magical time for my grieving to end.

My first big holiday without Von was Thanksgiving Day. Everybody was to meet at my parents' house, but I was still devastated and isolated myself from family gatherings. My mom called and asked me to come over to eat with the family. I really did not desire to go out, nor did I have an appetite. However, because my mom asked me, I went to be with my family. Everyone was there eating and enjoying themselves. When mom placed my plate before me at the table, I broke down and started crying. I could not eat, even though Mom wanted me to eat. I got up from the table and returned home. I had to deal with my grief day by day, and sometimes moment by moment, because I knew I had to live for my daughter and grandson. My commitment to God and Faith in God was maintain unshakeable in this valley experience.

There are times, we do not understand the ways of God, but we must trust Him. God leaves us with so many unanswered questions. Yet I had to remind myself that God will never leave me alone during my time of loss. Job said it best: "But He knows the way that I take [and He pays attention to it]. When He has tried me, I will come forth as [reined] gold [pure and luminous] (Job 23:10 AMP). First Corinthians 10:13 (KJV) says it this way: "There hath no temptation taken you but such as is common to man; but God is faithful, who will not suffer you to be tempted above that ye are able; But will with the temptation also make a way to escape, that ye may be able to bear it."

God's grace and mercies, along with the love of the saints, conditioned me to endure this test. During my grieving process, I recalled days and nights holding on to Travis's clothes just to smell his scent. Grasping his belongings gave me a sense of holding on to him. Absolutely no one knew the sleepless nights and the tears I endured. My tears were my meat because I could not eat. I found myself bouncing from sadness to anger, from anger to guilt, from guilt to sadness, and repeating the cycle. I would put this spiritual face on when visitors would come over, but I returned to my son's bedroom crying. My son left me a large insurance policy, but money could not fill this void in my heart. Visitors would come over to comfort and try to console me, and I appreciated them all, but it could not alleviate the pain. I can admit that if I did not have God in my life and spiritual people speaking into my life, I would have lost my mind. Because I worked in the mental health and substance abuse profession, I was familiar with the benefits of professional counseling. I took advantage of the services in addition to spiritual counseling. I had to hold on to the prophetic Word I preached the night he died: "I'm going through, but I am coming out with more than what I had," because I could not see how I was going to live without Travis.

One day I had a divine visitation from God's ministering angels, or God Himself, while in my prayer closet. In such a time as this, I chose the lowest place in my house as an act of humility to cry out before God for healing. I felt a heavy presence of God embracing me and bringing a spirit of peace upon me. While on that floor crying out before God, I recalled the Word of God ministering to me: "I will never leave you nor forsake you." As I began to travail in the spirit from my belly and speak in my heavenly language, I sensed the Holy Spirit making intercession for me. My Mediator, my Lord and Savior Jesus Christ, was interceding for me and presented the infirmities of my heart before the throne of God. As the Word of God declared in Romans 8:26 (KJV), "Likewise the Spirit also helpeth our infirmities: for we know not what we should pray for as we ought: but the Spirit itself maketh intercession for us with groanings which cannot be uttered."

Dr. Christine Landry Elliott

When I came to myself, I felt a supernatural deliverance within my soul and spirit. I believed the warring anointing upon my life had arrested the demonic forces that had overtaken my mind and spirit and lifted the spirit of depression. I felt a bounce-back anointing and a mighty breakthrough. I was able to exhale in the spirit, lifting the name of my Lord, Jesus Christ. God is my Jehovah Rapha; He is my Healer. Glory to God for restoration!

CHAPTER 14

From Glory to Glory

ONE OF MY FAVORITE VERSES IN THE BIBLE IS ROMANS 8:18 (KJV), "FOR I reckon that the sufferings of this present time are not worthy to be compared with the glory which shall be revealed in us." About six months after burying my son, I began to snap back into the flow of life after having a supernatural encounter with God in my prayer closet. The glory of God came in the room and rested upon me. I felt a refreshing and a restoration in my spirit, even though I was still going through a grieving process. I had to face the hardest celebratory holidays without Travis: Thanksgiving, Christmas, and his birthday, March 6. I did not do anything but return to work after a couple of weeks. It was about six months before I accepted preaching engagements again.

My pastor, the late Bishop Townsend, asked me to come to preach at my home church on a Sunday night. Remember, this is the same place I had been preaching when my son had died on that unforgettable Sunday night. I had high respect for my spiritual father and believed there was a reason he asked me to come at that appointed time. I trusted the leading of God in his life and accepted the preaching assignment. In fact, this was the first preaching engagement since I had buried my son. People were there to give me support, including my family. I'm sure there were people who only attended the service to see if I was going to have an emotional breakdown, but God held me together even as I testified about the loss of my son. I recalled struggling to bring my thoughts together while ministering the Word of God. I thought I was healed enough to minister, but it was obvious I was still grieving. The folks at church loved and embraced me. My mom's presence gave me extra strength to complete that assignment.

After delivering the Word of God, one of my spiritual sisters came to me in love and said, "I could tell you were struggling through your message." I considered why my bishop had asked me to preach, and I concluded that he felt it was time for me to get back on my divine assignment. What better place to relaunch my ministry than at my home church, under the covering of my spiritual father and my godmother, Mama Lottie. As an evangelist, I knew my assignment and purpose: it was always about winning souls for the kingdom of God. I started accepting preaching engagements and women's conferences, and I did empowerment sessions. At my regular job, I received a promotion and a salary increase. I became a certified substance abuse therapist and later received my license as an addiction specialist from the State of North Carolina.

Although my son was gone, he left his seed to continue his legacy. Praise God! Even though my son's father was in prison, which prohibited him from supporting Travis, by law Slim still had legal rights to receive a percentage of the insurance money and all his possessions. Slim had been in prison for twenty years. He shared regret about not raising his son, and he was very remorseful. He articulated how he respect and appreciation he had for me rearing our son to become a productive young man. Slim said, "I will not take any of the insurance money because I am unworthy." He wrote a letter to the courts waiving all parental rights to receive any of Travis's possessions or insurance money. I respected his decision. The love of God led me to send him a small percentage of the money considering he was sentence to 120 years in prison. In the year of 2015, Slim died in prison.

I crossed paths again with my former parole officer, Mr. Green, the man who had the power to revoke my parole and send me back to prison but released me. He showed up at the substance abuse facility where I was employed. We embraced and shared our stories since we had last spoken. He informed me that he had left the court system and was seeking employment in the substance abuse field. The table had turned, and God afforded me the opportunity to be able to help him. I shared my professional skills, influence, and support in assisting him in becoming a substance abuse counselor. I would always tell him how grateful I was to have him in my life and now in my story. We vowed that we would always be friends.

The Lord blessed me to become a homeowner and to purchase a new car. There were so many more blessings that God afforded me because of continuous prayer and perseverance through the storms of life. Hallelujah! The ministry was growing, and the demands for revivals had increased. The glory of God would show up everywhere I had to preach.

My daughter and I have reconciled, and we continue to work on our mother-daughter relationship. I count myself truly bless to still have Tee and my grandson with me after the death of Travis. God changed her plans to return to Camp Lejeune with Travis on the night of the accident. The devil's plan was to kill all my seeds. She has birthed me four grandsons, whom I love very much. During all the losses I suffered, I still saw the goodness and the blessings of the Lord in my life.

I thank God that I held on to my faith and refused to allow the enemy to hold me hostage to my past. My love for God never wavered, and Jehovah rewarded me for my faithfulness. I met a born-again gentleman name George, who I married in the year of 1996. He has enhanced and impact my life on a personal and spiritual level. We both were licensed addiction specialists by the North Carolina Licensed Substance Abuse and Mental Health Services. We became entrepreneurs in the field of our profession as the owners and private providers of Substance Abuse and DWI Service Businesses, with two locations in North Carolina. We were instrumental in helping families and witness lives transformed that brought forth reconciliation and healing. My husband and I became pastors and founders of a small church. God led my husband to name our ministry, Agape Christian Worship Center. I am a witness and a testimony that God can bring one's life from the pit to the palace. Praise God for Grace and Mercy!

My life's journey was necessary as a pathway to bridge me to my kingdom purpose and assignment. I conclude with the Word according to Romans 8:18 (KJV), "For I reckon that the sufferings of this present time are not worthy to be compared with the glory which shall be revealed in us." God has crowned my life with His glory! I give God all the glory and praise.

About the Author

Doctor Christine Landry Elliott is a native of Fayetteville, North Carolina. She is the daughter of the late Harold Landry and Ruth Landry. Christine is the oldest of seven siblings, which include her deceased brother Jeffery Landry and deceased sister Gwen Landry.

She accepted Christ as her Savior at the age of twenty-five and became active in church and committed to her faith. She began her ministry as a missionary in 1984. Christine preached across states in the United States, witnessing souls saved and delivered.

Christine graduated from Fayetteville State University and obtained a bachelor's degree in psychology. After obtaining her bachelor's degree, she pursued employment in the mental health and substance abuse field. Christine worked in the substance abuse field for over twenty-five years. She earned her master's degree in counseling in 2004 from Webster University, located in Myrtle Beach, South Carolina. Christine obtained her doctoral degree in ministry from Andersonville Theological Seminary in Camellia, Georgia.

Her passion is serving God's people through modeling a holy lifestyle, revelatory knowledge, and kingdom and practical principles. Her driven purpose is to win souls for the kingdom of God through ministry and being a light to those in darkness.

Christine has impacted, empowered, influenced, and inspired so many people during her time in ministry. Souls have accepted Christ, delivered from demonic strongholds, and healed through her preaching the Word of God and from hearing her powerful and overcoming testimonies.

Christine has dedicated the remaining years of her life on earth to serve God's people in various capacities, help others discover their kingdom purpose, and inspire them to pursue their dreams according to God's divine will.

Printed in the United States
by Baker & Taylor Publisher Services